W9-DCV-958

MOUNTAIN FOLKS

Fragments of Central Pennsylvania Lore

Other Publications by Homer T. Rosenberger

Testing Occupational Training and Experience. Published by United States Department of Justice, 1948.

Selection and Training of Personnel for Penal and Correctional Institutions in the United States Federal Prison System. Published by The United Nations, 1955.

What Should We Expect of Education? Published by the National Education Association (National Association of Secondary-School Principals), 1956.

How to Organize and Administer an Employee Training Program: A Manual for Executives and Training Directors. Published by Society for Personnel Administration, 1956.

Stimulating the Will to Learn: Employee Training Incentives, A Manual for Executives and Training Directors. Published by Society for Personnel Administration, 1958.

Techniques for Getting Things Done, Seventh Edition. Published by United States Department of Commerce, 1964.

Letters From Africa. Published by the American Peace Society, 1965.

The Pennsylvania Germans, 1891-1965. Published by the Pennsylvania German Society, 1966.

Adventures and Philosophy of a Pennsylvania Dutchman, An Autobiography in a Broad Setting. Published by Pennsylvania Heritage, Inc., 1971.

Man and Modern Society, Philosophical Essays. Published by Pennsylvania Heritage, Inc., 1972.

and more than three hundred and fifty articles, forewords, book reviews, courses, reports, and the like, most of them in professional journals or issued as U. S. Government documents.

MOUNTAIN FOLKS

Fragments of Central Pennsylvania Lore

by

HOMER TOPE ROSENBERGER, PH.D., LL.D.

Pen and Ink Sketches by Charles J. Stoner

ANNIE HALENBAKE ROSS LIBRARY
Lock Haven, Pennsylvania

1974

ISBN 0-915258-02-1

Library of Congress Catalog Card No. 73-85619

To The Memory Of Roy Glen Rich, 1893-1970

Remarkable Link

Between Mountain And Valley

FOREWORD

All literature is a reflection of life; its great value is to extend, expand, elaborate, investigate and illuminate experience. Its poignant effect comes from the ability of authors, poets, dramatists, essayists, biographers and historians to distil the essence of some aspect of human activity into a written record of shared adventure, through their observation and understanding, the insights of their imagination, the perceptiveness of their viewpoints and their skill in the use of language. They give us what they, as particularly sensitive individuals, have seen and heard and comprehended in their experience of life. They pass on what they have learned about humanity and what is called the "human condition."

There is a branch of literature, perhaps the oldest branch—perhaps the original trunk of the tree—which is not so much individual and personal, like most prose and poetry, but more a common inheritance handed on from one to another from a receding past. The literature of folklore is not the work of self-conscious authors and artists. Rather, it is the essence of certain human attitudes shared by closeknit groups, in gossip, in story-telling, in social intercourse, in all the many ways in which people pass on to one another the ideas, emotions and feelings they have together as they are born, grow up, grow old and die, sharing a time and a place. Such conceptions, responses, reactions and imaginings are collected into the heritage of a tribe, a community, a society, as odds and ends are piled into an old-fashioned scrap-dealer's cart, with some new artifact adding variety to the cargo at every wayside and cross-roads encounter.

Folklore has been inherited more by word of mouth than by the written record; it has come to us from generations of talkers, story-tellers and tale-spinners; it is not the fruit of a unique literary genius nor any "school" of writers.

The interplay of human communication which results in folklore is informal, almost spontaneous, by contrast with the personal stimulation and interchange that has occurred, throughout the history of the novel, the short story, the epic and the lyric, among writers who have influenced each other by emulation, rivalry, congeniality, friendship and competition, making rules to which they hold each other and those who come after, establishing conventions to bind their followers. There is none of that to hamper the makers of folklore. They take what came to them, add to it what they want to give, and let it float on to the next generation of story-tellers.

The telling of tales to explain the mysteries of nature, the puzzles of strange phenomena in the skies, the mountains, the woods, the rivers, the seas, and in the behavior of human beings, in infancy, in old age, in love and war, in work and play, in the security of home and in the fear of strangers, is as old as speech; older, no doubt, than cave paintings and carved inscriptions.

One can easily imagine how superstitions, religious beliefs, traditional taboos and rites of behavior, had their origin from the same human impulses as folklore, as men and women and their children lived together in primitive communities, haphazardly stumbling on some of the truths of geography, astronomy, psychology, and physics. One can see how the inheritance of each generation carried an increase of legend as well as truth, as elders handed down to their children what they had discovered, of science or superstition, in their lifetime.

Folklore was the treasure trove accumulated from the human impulse toward fun, laughter and entertainment, as well as the wonderment which must have stimulated the primitive imagination to provide an explanation for every paradox in the unexplored and still mysterious physical world, and the even more mysterious and fascinating world of human relationships.

This is why folklore is like fossil rock. Imbedded in the tale handed down from the past are traces of the life of human beings in ages gone.

Such tales must have undergone many changes, from the pressures of time and historical upheaval. They contain the intriguing remains of human speculations, social traditions, ways of thinking and feeling, habits of thought and behavior, which once helped mankind to survive in a rigorous world, and have themselves survived into a time which is very different, yet wonderously a continuation, from some far-distant age.

Central Pennsylvania contains many strains of folklore, for this commonwealth has drawn its people from a wide area of the earth over the span of three centuries. They have brought together in the three great river valley systems of Pennsylvania a fascinating variety of the old tales ingrown groups of people have developed as part of their protection against natural forces they could not trust, control or understand. As the events of history have moved people from one place to another, the baggage they have always carried with them has included the invisible touchstone of folklore. The people who emigrated into Pennsylvania, from the start, brought with them their folk beliefs, along with the family treasures, the souvenirs of their old life, and the tools for crafts and skills which a wayfarer carries to make his way in new surroundings.

It is our misfortune, of course, that no one can really glean the full harvest of the old stories, songs and traditions which comprise even one inheritance of folklore. These things vanish and may be lost with the passage of time, like the old tools, the obsolete household implements, the bunchy bustles and brocaded waistcoats, which ultimately may survive only in museums, sometimes marked with a card to say that, now, no one knows just how this article was used once upon a time.

Fortunately, however, there have been careful and dedicated researchers in the field of folklore, who have gathered up a significant fragment of what was once a rich hoard of the accretions of folk history. That which they have found and recorded is giving us a new dimension of our broader history. We are gaining an insight into the ways of our ancestors which is not part of the record of their political and military battles, nor their formal recollections of their times. In the folk tales which have been resurrected from the memories of old story tellers we have a unique means of direct contact with the past.

The people who heard folk stories from their parents and grandparents, who heard them from generations beyond, and who passed them on to modern listeners, had no incentive to put a fine face on anything. They simply tried to recall what they once heard as a part of the life that their forebears knew. What they pass on through this channel has a significance which does not lie in the quaint turns of phrase in which the tale may be told, nor in any pedantic bibliography which says, "This story was told to me by Aunt Jessie Sourbranch who heard it from her grandfather, who said it was a story he was told by the one-time slave his Aunt Fanny brought up from Georgia on a visit to his daddy's farm near Shippensburg".

Dialect and genealogy have their importance in the collecting of folklore just as it is interesting to know where Shakespeare got the stories he wove into his great dramas. But the ultimate significance of folktales is what they tell us about the persistence of ideas and notions. Many versions of the same romantic plot may crop up in the word-of-mouth tales handed down in half a dozen different folk-groups.

Herein lies the virtue of this book of Homer T. Rosenberger's, in which he has recreated for Central Pennsylvanians some of the moods and sentiments which animated their forebears in a simpler time, but in this very place. Reading these stories, sometimes wondering how they got started and what transformations they went through as they made their way down to us, one begins to feel a kinship with the people who whiled away their leisure hours with the telling of such tales, some of them well recognized as "tall stories," both then and now. They bring to us some glimpse of what it was like to live an isolated frontier life, and what one generation got from another as village and farm society and life in lumber camps and on the river, evolved into the sophisticated industrial society of today.

"Mountain Folks" will save fragments of the central Pennsylvania mountain inheritance from forgetfulness and will shed some new light on it. These recollections of what people were like in the earlier, simpler days in Central Pennsylvania are more than a random footnote to our history.

These stories of the mountain folks are worth preserving and deserve reading, study and remembering, as part of the background we all share, whether we be sixth generation descendants of the first "Pennsylvania Dutch" farmers who responded to William Penn's search for people to till the rich soil of Penn's Woods, or recent arrivals who want to know some of the traditions we may share as newer Pennsylvanians. Here are stories of the people who made the history of this central section of Pennsylvania, in human terms, as canal boatmen, as raftmen and lumbermen, as farmers and blacksmiths, carpenters and masons, but most of all as those who made the mountains part of the life of Pennsylvania.

The Annie Halenbake Ross Library of Lock Haven believes that a library must do more in its community than provide a waystation for the exchanging of books. We are proud to be able to cooperate with Dr. Rosenberger in bringing this useful, entertaining, and significant book into being. We believe it will bring pleasure to many and add a significant volume to the books which describe Pennsylvania and Pennsylvanians.

The Board of Trustees of the Ross Library particularly wishes to add an expression of gratitude to Dr. Rosenberger, for his gifts of the manuscript of "Mountain Folks," to the illustrator, Mr. Charles J. Stoner for the effective art work he has contributed, to Mr. George Swetnam for his chapters on the folklore of lumbering, and to Mr. M. P. Hartzell, Plant Superintendent, Times and News Publishing Company, Gettysburg, Pennsylvania, for bringing all this into a handsome book.

Rebecca F. Gross
President, Board of Trustees
Annie Halenbake Ross Library
Lock Haven, Pa.

Preface

This volume reproduces fifteen articles comprising a series, "Clinton County Folklore," which I wrote in 1934 and in 1935. The articles are reprinted, here, almost exactly as they were published in the *Clinton County Weekly*, Lock Haven, Pennsylvania, between May 4, 1934, and March 15, 1935. Five of the articles were reprinted in the *Keystone Folklore Quarterly*, volume II, Winter 1957-1958, no. 4, pages 104-108, volume III, Spring 1958, no. 1, pages 2-4, volume III, Summer 1958, no. 2, pages 42-45, volume III, Fall 1958, no. 3, pages 75-80, and volume IV, Spring-Summer 1959, nos. 1 and 2, pages 121-126. In this book the fifteen articles are placed in a broader setting than previously, through the insertion of five introductory chapters.

The fifteen articles are accompanied by two somewhat similar articles written by Dr. George Swetnam, well-known folklorist and historian who was a feature writer for the *Pittsburgh Press* from 1943 to 1974. Both of Dr. Swetnam's articles deal with Central Pennsylvania and are reproduced here with his permission.

As described in the book *Adventures and Philosophy of a Pennsylvania Dutchman, An Autobiography in a Broad Setting*, 1971, Chapter Seven, "Mystery Man of Pine Mountain," I wrote the series of folklore articles while living in Clinton County from October 1932 until August 1935 among the people on the top of the Bald Eagle Mountain. I admired those people and they opened their hearts. Even with the recording equipment available in the early 1930's it would have been difficult to capture by mechanical means the real spirit of those people. Some would have "shyed" away from the recording equipment. A few would have given an exaggerated impression, either slyly or in jest. Living among those mountain folks proved to be an effective way to understand their view of life.

In those years, 1932-1935, I gathered the material for the articles. I was observing a way of life that would soon change rapidly and was probably collecting the last shreds of quaint and delightful folktales of that area. Those tales, handed orally from generation to generation, have since evaporated. Improved roads, electric lines, and the radio and television have penetrated the back country.

A thorough study of the lore of the mountain folks in Central Pennsylvania would have required a score of years of full-time effort prior to 1935. It is too late to make such a study, for we now live in a day of homogenization. This book deals only with part of the folklife and some of the folktales of the mountain people, and mainly in Clinton County. Nevertheless, the folklife and folktales prior to 1935 of the people in the remote parts of Clinton County were no doubt very similar to those of their contemporaries in numerous other secluded parts of the mountains of Central Pennsylvania.

With the perspective of forty years since the series of fifteen articles was first published it appears that the series makes an original contribution to the folklore of mountain people in Central Pennsylvania.

By the time the fifteenth article in that series was written I was already deep into research concerning the history of Pennsylvania. Beginning to take the view that folklore is unscientific and that history can be documented precisely, I abandoned the writing of folklore and concentrated upon history. With the perspective of the additional years I still believe that folklore as it is frequently written is far from scientific but have also found that the writing of history frequently is not nearly as scientific as it is thought to be. In looking back at the folklore articles of 1934 and 1935 I am now convinced that they are an accurate portrayal of part of the way of life of men, women, and children who lived in the mountains of Central Pennsylvania from approximately 1885 to 1935, and that, therefore, those articles should be republished. The 1973 printing of *A Guide for Collectors Of Oral Traditions and Folk Cultural Material In Pennsylvania* states that few folktales from Pennsylvania have been published. (Page 11). The *Guide* was written by MacEdward Leach and Henry Glassie and was published by the Pennsylvania Historical and Museum Commission.

Many of the illustrations in this book were reproduced from rare photographs and one from a tintype, gathered jointly by Mr. Franklin A. Rich and Mrs. Mary Sour Gardner, both of whom live in Wayne Township, Clinton County, within the shadow of the Bald Eagle Mountain, Mrs. Gardner at Pine Station and Mr. Rich two miles west, both on Rural Route 1, Lock Haven. Some of the illustrations were reproduced from photographs taken in 1973 and 1974 by Mr. Rich. A number were reproduced from photograph collections in the Archives Tower in Harrisburg through the courtesy of Dr. Donald H. Kent, Director, Bureau of Archives and History, Pennsylvania Historical and Museum Commission, and Mr. Harold L. Myers, Associate Historian, Bureau of Archives and History, Pennsylvania Historical and Museum Commission. Five of the illustrations were reproduced from photographs taken in August 1973 at the Annual Woodsmen's Carnival held at the Pennsylvania Lumber Museum in Potter County. Those photographs were taken by Mr. Michael J. Ripton, Director, Bureau of Historic Sites and Properties, Pennsylvania Historical and Museum Commission.

Four maps are included. Two concern parts of Clinton County. There is also a relief map of Pennsylvania, and an outline map of the State. The latter shows the boundary of each county, the name and location of each county seat, and the area referred to in this book as "Central Pennsylvania."

The folktales in this book are brought back to life, dramatically, by thirty-two superb pen and ink sketches by Mr. Charles J. Stoner of Mercersburg, Pennsylvania, who lives near the foot of one of Central Pennsylvania's grandest mountains, the Tuscarora. Mr. Stoner's sketches help greatly to preserve the warmth and vividness of these tales. To him I am deeply indebted for his artistic renditions and for his insistence that the articles should be available in book form.

May 10, 1974 H. T. R.
Rose Hill
Waynesboro, Pa.

Mountains and the gorges and valleys between them constitute the most picturesque characteristic of Central Pennsylvania. The sturdy and resourceful people who lived in remote parts of those mountains in the nineteenth century and early in the twentieth, away from the cities, towns, and villages in the valleys, were an interesting segment of the population of the United States. Today the way of life and the tales told by those mountain folks are scarcely more than a memory, but are extremely fascinating.

Contents

Illustrations

PAGE

Penn's Majestic Mountains

Mountains in Pennsylvania and elsewhere are majestic except in those instances when they are scarred by human effort, carelessness, or vandalism. Mountains have a mystical and an almost awesome quality. They enrich the horizon. The sheer size of a mountain is overpowering. Mountains have been a symbol of strength from Old Testament times, and a symbol of beauty for centuries.

Even though geologists tell us that mountains were formed either as wrinkles when the earth's hot crust began to cool, or as the result of erosion after many hundreds of years of rain and wind, we still marvel that the mountains were created. Also, we realize that man, with enormous quantities of mechanical power at his command, has never built a large mountain, nor a beautiful one.

Of course, not everyone has a deep-rooted appreciation for mountains. In the 1950's at the Pennsylvania State University at State College in Centre County the Vice President for Research loved the mountains that flanked the campus, Nittany Mountain on the east and Bald Eagle Mountain on the west. He enjoyed telling about his brother's visit to the town of State College and the campus. His brother lived in Illinois and had never been in the East. He arrived in the town of State College at night. The next morning the man from the Illinois tableland looked about and remarked that State College would be an attractive place were it not for the mountains cutting off the view!

What surpasses the view of mountains from the very top of one of them? Is there any grandeur that equals a sunrise or a sunset in mountainous country? And how can one ever forget the variety of plant life, birds, and game, the sparkling springs of pure water, and the dashing cascades that are found on a mountainside?

Mountain folks in Central Pennsylvania or almost anywhere else are a sturdy clan. People living in remote parts of the Appalachians in Eastern United States or in the Rockies, Cascades, or Sierra Nevadas in the American West have a way of life that attracts much attention. However, the number of remote areas in the United States is dwindling rapidly.

For centuries the people living in the Bavarian Alps in Southeastern Germany, in the high hinterland of India and Afghanistan, and in other mountainous parts of the world have followed a strenuous and rather restricted but fascinating life style.

In any country, mountain folks live close to nature. In general they are resourceful and hospitable. The assembly line does not rule their lives but the computer is beginning to reach them. Because of their relative isolation they cling to tradition. But so do other people. Their way of life changes less rapidly than does the way of life in towns and cities. Nevertheless, mountain folks, of course, always had many of the same qualities, drives, and frustrations found among their contemporaries in the fertile valleys or close to seaports, or in cities on the great plains in North and South America and in Africa and on the steppes of Russia and Asia.

In any part of the world, mountain folks seem to have fewer advantages, in some respects, than other people. Due to erosion, mountain soil is seldom of high quality. Those who make their living from the soil must be sturdy in order to survive on poor soil. The everyday services found in cities are few in a remote mountain area because it is too expensive to furnish those services for only a handful of persons per square mile. Until recently in Central Pennsylvania transportation was awkward in remote mountain areas, schooling was somewhat neglected, and medical assistance was difficult to procure in an emergency. Rural delivery of mail did not reach into those remote areas. Telephone and electric lines were only a dream of things to come. Nevertheless, mountain folks in Central Pennsylvania and mountain folks in many parts of the world survived all of these disadvantages, and, in general, probably lived as long as the people in the valleys. The mountain folks in Central Pennsylvania in the days of comparative isolation, up to about 1940, were approximately as sturdy in health and in spirit as the remainder of the population of the middle third of the State.

As used in this book, the words Central Pennsylvania refer to the middle third of the State, from the Mason and Dixon line to the New York boundary.

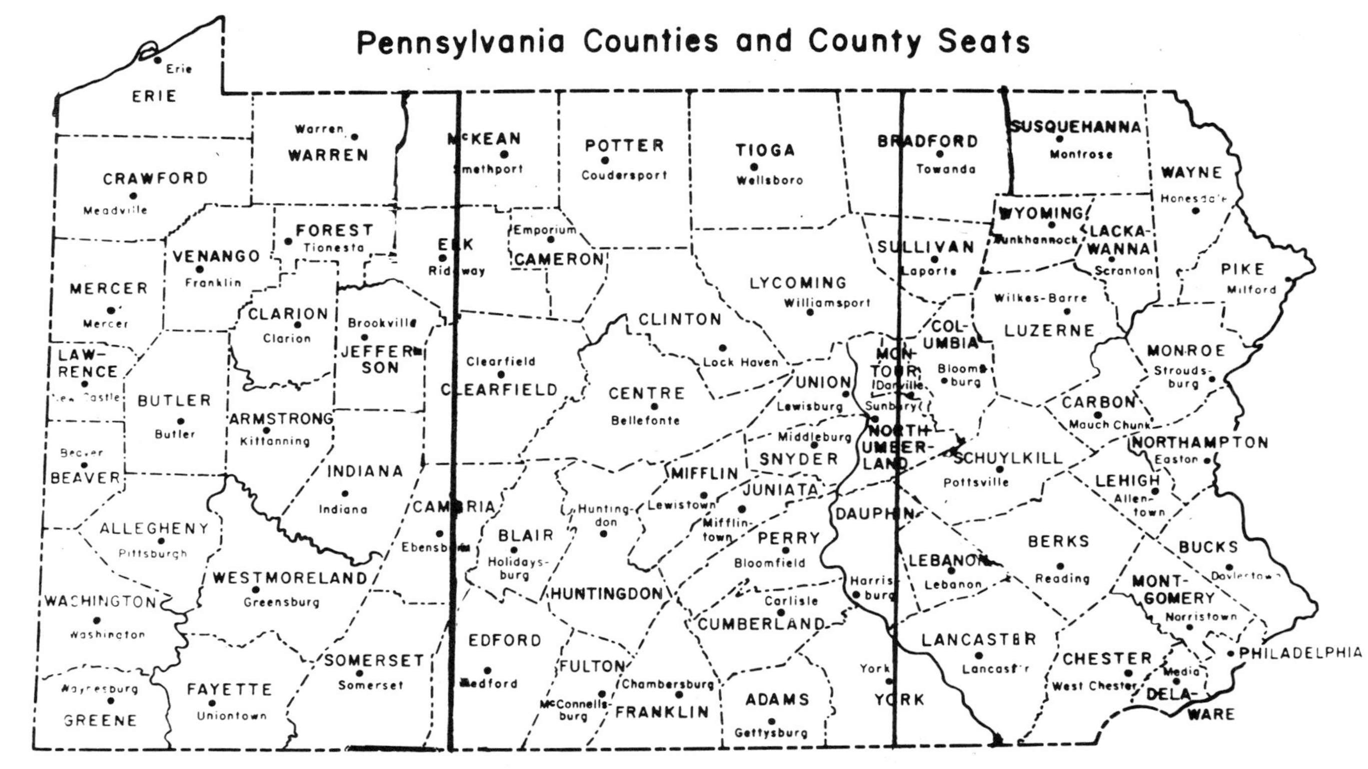

OUTLINE MAP OF CENTRAL PENNSYLVANIA

The middle third of Pennsylvania embraces three counties along the Mason and Dixon line, Adams, Franklin, and Fulton, and parts of two others, York and Bedford, and two counties along the New York line, Tioga and Potter, and parts of two others, Bradford and McKean, and the counties between those nine. That middle third forms a vertical rectangle.

Central Pennsylvania is blessed with majestic mountains interspersed with beautiful valleys. One of its grandest mountains is the Bald Eagle, in the scenic ridge and valley region, an area which forms a wide arc. Parallel mountains and valleys extend from the Maryland line in a curve toward the northeast, to the anthracite fields. Many of the boundaries of Central Pennsylvania counties in this ridge and valley region follow the ridges.

The ridge and valley region is heavily wooded. Some of its valleys are wide and are underlaid with limestone, have been farmed productively from colonial times, and are used extensively today for dairy farming. Among these productive limestone areas are Morrison's Cove, and Nittany, Kishacoquillas, Penn's, Brush, Sugar, and Nippenose Valleys. However, many of the valleys in the ridge and valley region of Central Pennsylvania are narrow and are shale, usually having thin soil. In parts of the shale valleys farms have been abandoned and the forest is returning.

THE MOUNTAINS OF CENTRAL PENNSYLVANIA—RELIEF MAP

This relief map shows the ridge and valley region of South Central Pennsylvania, with the mountains curving northeast from the Mason and Dixon line. A high tableland, the Allegheny Plateau, extends into much of the western part of North Central Pennsylvania. Southeastern Pennsylvania is little above sea level and is a land of rolling hills.

Early in the nineteenth century much charcoal iron was manufactured in the valleys of the ridge and valley region. The enormous amount of wood from which to make charcoal for fuel, large deposits of limestone to be used for flux in the furnaces, and many pockets of iron ore were found in close proximity to each other.

Even though much of the ridge and valley region is not heavily populated it has a number of prosperous cities and towns, including Bedford, Altoona, Huntingdon, Tyrone, Bellefonte, State College, Lewistown, Lewisburg, Lock Haven, Williamsport, Bloomsburg, and Berwick.

Immediately to the west of the ridge and valley region there are two Bald Eagle Creeks originating near each other, at the foot of the Bald Eagle Mountain. The one flows southwest about twenty miles to the Juniata River at Tyrone. The other flows through the Bald Eagle Valley for nearly fifty miles, northeast, entering the West Branch of the Susquehanna at Lock Haven.

The Bald Eagle Mountain extends from Tyrone, on the Juniata River, to Muncy, on the West Branch of the Susquehanna River, a distance of about eighty-five miles. The mountain forms something like a semi-circle and is broken by gaps, frequently from three to seven miles apart. Immediately east of Lock Haven the mountain is buttressed by spurs and high tableland, making it approximately twelve miles wide in that part of Clinton County, and a delightful wilderness area.

The Bald Eagle Mountain, Bald Eagle Valley, the Bald Eagle Creek that flows northeast to Lock Haven, and Bald Eagle Township in Clinton County were each named for Delaware Indian Chief, Wapalanné, or Bald Eagle. Also, the Bald Eagle Creek that flows southwest to the Juniata River was probably named for him. Chief Bald Eagle's town was on the Bald Eagle Creek approximately one mile below the confluence of Bald Eagle and Spring Creeks, near Milesburg in Centre County. His wigwam was located between two white oaks and his town was known in the colonial records of Pennsylvania as "the Bald Eagle's nest." It is believed that he was killed in 1779 near Brady's Bend, on the Allegheny River, by the Indian fighter, Samuel Brady.

The Clearfield County bituminous coal fields and much of the eastern beginnings of the Allegheny Plateau lie adjacent to and west of the Bald Eagle Valley.

The Black Forest, an interesting wilderness in southern Potter County and in parts of Tioga, Lycoming, Clinton, and Cameron Counties, was approximately forty miles square—nearly a million acres—prior to extensive lumbering. The center of the Black Forest was about thirty-five miles northwest of Lock Haven. In mid nineteenth century the Black Forest had such heavy stands of choice white pine and hemlock that it was difficult for the sun's rays to penetrate those stands to the forest floor on the brightest days. There were mature stands of white, pitch, and shortleaf pines, oak, and chestnut on the higher elevations and fine stands of pine, hemlock, beech, birch, maple, basswood, and cherry on the slopes and in the lower areas.

A ballad that was a favorite in the lumber camps of the Black Forest of Pennsylvania included the following stanza:

> Wherever you may wander,
> And taste the nation's bounty,
> You'll find there is no place on earth
> Like good old Potter County.

This stanza, under the caption "Roving Jo," is found in *North Pennsylvania Minstrelsy*, edition of 1919, by Henry Wharton Shoemaker, page 158.

CAMP LIFE IN THE BLACK FOREST IN 1895

When lumbering was at its height in Pennsylvania, about 1880-1900, lumberjacks lived in camps in the mountains, the camps being located in the area where the men were felling trees. Less frequently lumberjacks took their families with them into the woods. Here we see mountain folks living in primitive fashion.

The scenic Pine Creek Gorge, "Pennsylvania's Grand Canyon," in Tioga County, is east of the Black Forest and is about forty miles north of Lock Haven. The gorge is so narrow that the New York Central Railroad track (Penn Central in 1974) barely squeezes in beside the stream.

PENNSYLVANIA'S GRAND CANYON

Pine Creek Gorge in Tioga County. View looking south toward Lock Haven, from Leonard Harrison State Park. From a photograph taken on the evening of August 19, 1946.

Immediately to the east of Pennsylvania's ridge and valley region is the broad and fertile Cumberland Valley. It extends from the Maryland line to Harrisburg, and almost joins the Lebanon Valley which reaches from Harrisburg to Reading, and from which there is easy access along the Blue Mountain to Allentown and the Lehigh Valley. Thus a great arched corridor flanks the mountains of Central Pennsylvania. The corridor reaches from the Mason and Dixon line to a point on the Delaware River fifty-seven miles above Philadelphia.

Useful facts concerning the geography of Central Pennsylvania are given in a simple way in the following four books, the first of which was published much over a century ago.

Charles B. Trego. *A Geography Of Pennsylvania: Containing An Account Of The History, Geographical Features, Soil, Climate, Geology, Botany, Zoology, Population, Education, Government, Finances, Productions, Trade, Rail Roads, Canals, &c. Of The State; With A Separate Description Of Each County, And Questions For The Convenience Of Teachers. To Which Is Appended, A Travellers' Guide, Or Table Of Distances On The Principal Rail Road, Canal And Stage Routes In The State*. Philadelphia, 1843. Edward C. Biddle.

Part II of Trego's *Geography* contains the descriptions, county by county, thus providing much information, specifically, about Central Pennsylvania.

Zoe A. Thralls. *The Geography of Pennsylvania*. New York, 1926. Macmillan Company.

Raymond E. Murphy and Marion [F.] Murphy. *Pennsylvania, A Regional Geography*. Harrisburg, Pa., 1937. The Pennsylvania Book Service.

Raymond E. Murphy and Marion F. Murphy, *Pennsylvania Landscapes, A Geography of the Commonwealth*, Second edition, 1955, State College, Pa. Penns Valley Publishers, Inc.

Detailed studies of the geography of Central Pennsylvania have been made over a period of more than a century by geological survey teams employed by the State. Their studies of topography, minerals, mineral industries, and floods are available in book and pamphlet form. For example, Bulletin C 1, Pennsylvania Geological Survey, Fourth Series, is a cloth-bound book of 153 pages and two large folding maps, entitled *Geology and Mineral Resources of Adams County, Pennsylvania*. The study was published in 1932 by the Pennsylvania Department of Internal Affairs.

Central Pennsylvania's history is as rich as its terrain is rugged. Penn's majestic mountains are the locale of an abundant drama of eighteenth, nineteenth and twentieth century life. Indians played an important part in

MOUNTAINS IN THE WESTERN PART OF LYCOMING COUNTY

Scene from Cammal View Point. In foreground, the village of Cammal, and, difficult to distinguish, Pine Creek, and a branch of the New York Central Railroad, now the Penn Central. From a photograph taken September 18, 1939.

that history. Indian settlements such as those near Lock Haven, on Great Island in the West Branch of the Susquehanna River, and on nearby lowland on the south bank of the river, and Indian paths, such as the Kittanning Trail, across much of Pennsylvania, were of great significance.

The sites of numerous Indian villages in Central Pennsylvania have been located through archaeological investigation. In the summer of 1971 archaeologists on the staff of the Pennsylvania Historical and Museum Commission supervised the removal of topsoil by bulldozer from an area of approximately 25,000 square feet at the Quiggle Site, at Pine Station. After the archaeologists studied the subsoil at the site they found from the stains that there had been on this site a stockaded town built by the Susquehannock Indians about 1550 A. D. The town had been somewhat circular in shape, nearly 200 feet in diameter, surrounded by a single-line stockade or fence consisting of poles placed in the ground and lashed together to provide security for the inhabitants. There had been a shallow ditch around the outside of the stockade.

SITE OF SUSQUEHANNOCK INDIAN VILLAGE, PINE STATION

This is the Quiggle Site, in Clinton County. The line of short stakes in the picture shows the location of the village.

Indian title to Pennsylvania was extinguished by a series of thirty-three treaties and purchases, and various deeds received from Indians, from July 15, 1682, to March 3, 1792, a period of almost 110 years. Part of Central Pennsylvania was opened to white settlement in 1736, the part now comprising Adams, Franklin, and Cumberland Counties. In 1754 the area now embraced by Fulton, Bedford, Blair, Huntingdon, Perry, Juniata, Mifflin, and parts of Centre, Snyder, and Union Counties was opened to the white man. In 1768 land that now is included in parts of Clearfield, Centre, Clinton, Union, Northumberland, and Lycoming Counties was opened for settlement by white people. The remainder of Central Pennsylvania was opened for white settlement in 1784.

Between 1755 and 1764, during both the French and Indian War and Pontiac's Conspiracy, the Indians descended upon the white settlers in Central Pennsylvania and killed many, perhaps several hundred, took about 200 captive, and burned their houses and barns, and in some cases their crops in the fields. The settlers on Penns Creek in present Snyder County were attacked by Indians on October 16, 1755. About twenty were killed, wounded or carried away as captives. This Penns Creek "massacre" was followed by a series of outrages. Much has been written about Mary Jemison and Richard Bard who were taken captive by the Indians. Both lived in what is now Adams County.

BARD FAMILY CAPTURE AND BALLAD

Escape from the Indians—from the Ballad of Richard Bard

Richard Bard, his wife, and others were surprised by nineteen Indians on April 13, 1758, at the Bard home. Bard and eight other white persons were taken captive. Bard's home was burned by the Indians. Bard escaped but his wife was forced to walk more than 500 miles from time of the capture. After two years and five months she was reunited with her husband and they lived for many years near what is now the village of Upton in present Franklin County. A ballad of sixty-four stanzas of four lines each recounts the gruesome experience. The first stanza is as follows:

On a woeful day the heathen came,
And did us captives make;
And then the miseries commenced,
Of which we did partake.

The details of the capture and captivity of the Bard family, the escape of Richard Bard, and the reuniting of Bard and his wife are given in an article by Mrs. T. H. Krebs Benchoff, "The Ballad of Richard Bard—1758," together with the sixty-four stanzas. The article is found in *Kittochtinny Historical Society Papers*, volume XV, 1970, pages 1-11.

On July 26, 1764, a school teacher, Enoch Brown, and nine or more of his pupils were slain in Franklin County by Indians, at Brown's schoolhouse three-and-a-half miles northwest of present Greencastle.

In the immediate vicinity of Bedford the Indians killed, scalped, or took prisoner eighteen persons.

Forts built in Central Pennsylvania at time of the French and Indian War had an exciting history, as for example McDowell's Fort built in 1755 and Fort Loudoun built in 1756, both in present Franklin County and at the east foot of the Tuscarora Mountain. John McDowell's mill became Fort McDowell when stockaded in 1755 by McDowell and his neighbors, as a place of protection at time of raids by the Indians. The provincial authorities of Pennsylvania used Fort McDowell until construction of Fort Loudoun was begun the next year, approximately two-and-a-half miles northwest of Fort McDowell.

Fort Lyttelton, near the present town of Fort Littleton in Fulton County, was begun in December 1755 and was used by troops until 1760. Fort Bedford, first known as Raystown Fort, was built in 1758 on the Raystown Branch of the Juniata River. The fort was enlarged in 1759 and was renamed in honor of the Duke of Bedford in England. These forts were havens of refuge for the frontier settlers.

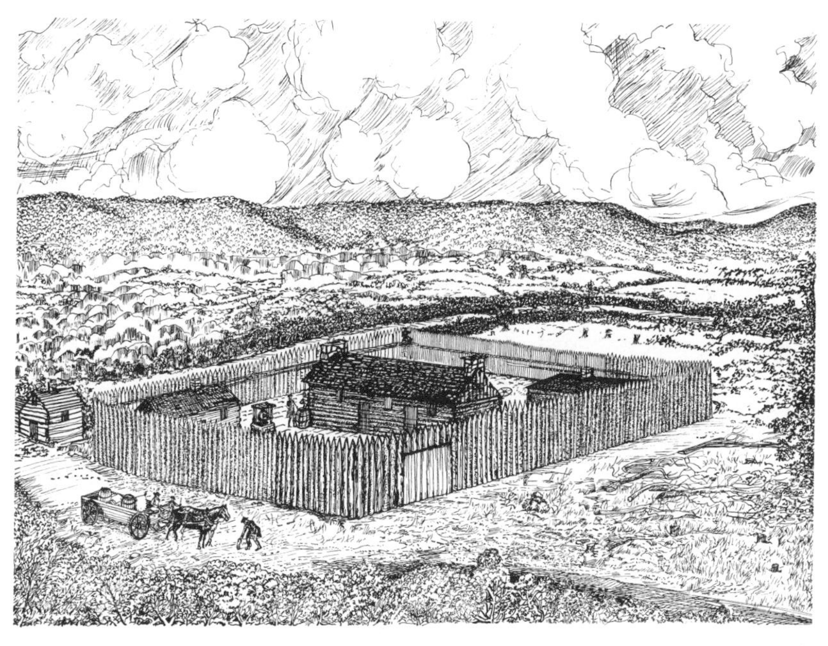

Fort McDowell

A pen and ink reconstruction by Charles J. Stoner

Some of the forts in Central Pennsylvania were besieged, such as Fort Granville built in 1755-1756 on a high bank of the Juniata River near the present site of Lewistown, Mifflin County. During the harvest of 1756 the garrison was in the grain fields protecting the settlers while gathering the crops. After the fort was attacked twice by Indians it was destroyed by them on July 30, 1756. The commander of the garrison at Fort Granville, Lieutenant Edward Armstrong, was killed. The entire garrison was either killed or taken captive. Fort Bedford was the starting point in 1758 of the Forbes Expedition against the French at Fort Duquesne, present Pittsburgh. At times more than a thousand troops were quartered at Fort Bedford.

In 1777, during the Revolution, there had been frequent Indian raids on the white settlers in the West Branch Valley. Almost immediately after the Wyoming Massacre on July 3, 1778, in Northeastern Pennsylvania, the settlers in the West Branch Valley left en masse, on rafts, in boats of various kinds, in canoes, and in almost anything on which they could float down the river. This flight of the settlers in 1778, to escape the Indians, is known as the Great Runaway. For the next five years it was unsafe for those settlers to return to their farms—until 1783. Also during the Revolution, the Bedford Scouts were ambushed on June 3, 1781, by Indians. The commander of the Scouts, Captain John Boyd, was taken prisoner, seventeen of the scouts were killed and scalped, and five were wounded. A monument near Altoona marks the site of the massacre.

Eighteenth century pioneer life in Central Pennsylvania, including the struggles with the Indians, was followed in the 19th by the extensive manufacture of charcoal iron, improvement of transportation, the conducting of lumbering on a large scale, and the expansion of agriculture and various kinds of manufacturing, as touched upon in the next chapter.

Facts concerning the history of Central Pennsylvania are given in an almost countless number of books and articles. Among the most useful books are the following. Sherman Day's *Historical Collections of the State of Pennsylvania*, 1843, and William H. Egle's *An Illustrated History of the Commonwealth of Pennsylvania, Civil, Political and Military, From Its Earliest Settlement to the Present Time*, 1876 and later editions. These two books consist mainly of a chapter devoted to each county of the State. Therefore an overall view of any county in Central Pennsylvania can be obtained quickly by consulting the appropriate chapter in either book.

I. D. Rupp wrote several volumes about Pennsylvania. One that was published in 1847 focuses on Central Pennsylvania. It is entitled *History and Topography of Northumberland, Huntingdon, Mifflin, Centre, Union, Columbia, Juniata and Clinton counties, Pa. Embracing Local And General Events, Leading Incidents, Descriptions Of The Principal*

Boroughs, Towns, Villages, Etc., Etc. With A Copious Appendix: Embellished By Engravings. Compiled From Authentic Sources. A companion volume by Rupp dealt with Dauphin, Cumberland, Franklin, Bedford, Adams, Perry, Somerset, Cambria, and Indiana Counties.

Two journalists each wrote an important early book about Central Pennsylvania. In 1856 Uriah J. Jones's *History of the Early Settlement of Juniata Valley* was published in Philadelphia. A new edition edited by Floyd G. Hoenstine was published in Harrisburg in 1940. John F. Meginness's *Otzinachson: A History of the West Branch Valley of the Susquehanna,* was published in Williamsport in 1889, as an extensive enlargement of his *Otzinachson* published in 1857.

John Blair Linn's *History of Centre and Clinton Counties, Pennsylvania,* 1883, and J. Simpson Africa's *History of Huntingdon and Blair Counties, Pennsylvania,* also published in 1883, are extremely helpful in gaining an understanding of those four counties in Central Pennsylvania.

Frederic A. Godcharles's *Chronicles of Central Pennsylvania,* four volumes, 1944, New York, Lewis Historical Publishing Company, is the most extensive single work dealing with the history of the middle third of the State.

A large number of books and articles relating to the history of the various counties, cities, and towns in Central Pennsylvania, are listed in *Bibliography of Pennsylvania History,* in a section extending from page 550 to page 632. That volume was compiled by Norman B. Wilkinson, edited by S. K. Stevens and Donald H. Kent, and published by the Pennsylvania Historical and Museum Commission in 1957.

II

Nineteenth Century Mountain Folks

The original white settlers of Central Pennsylvania in colonial times were hardy souls. Nearly all of them arrived from Eastern Pennsylvania. They came by way of the Juniata River, the West Branch of the Susquehanna River, and other watercourses, by whatever kind of hand-powered raft or boat they could acquire, or moved overland on Indian trails. They settled on the flat land at the confluence of streams. Those settlers were English, Scotch-Irish, and German. When Pennsylvania's canals were built in the period 1826-1840 Irish workmen came to Central Pennsylvania to dig the canals. Many of those Irish workmen remained and their descendants live in Central Pennsylvania in the 1970's.

As population grew in the middle portion of the State in the nineteenth century some of the more adventurous left the towns and the rural parts of the valleys and established themselves in the remote sections of the nearby mountains. Some men living in the mountains dug iron ore for the charcoal iron furnaces, some cut logs, piled them, covered them with ground and burned them to make charcoal that was hauled from the mountainsides to the furnaces as fuel.

The men who made charcoal for the furnaces assembled mounds of small logs and then covered the mounds with ground. The logs were burned slowly and thus turned into charcoal to be used as the fuel in blast furnaces where pig iron was made. Building a charcoal mound and burning it slowly required skill and judgment. The process is described by Jacob H. Stoner in *Historical Papers, Franklin County and the Cumberland Valley, Pennsylvania*, 1947, pages 157-159 and 545.

The manufacture of iron was an important industry in Central Pennsylvania during the first half of the nineteenth century and gave employment to numerous people living in remote places. In 1832 there were eight furnaces, ten forges, and one rolling and slitting mill in Huntingdon County and approximately the same number in Centre County. Eighteen years later, in 1850, Huntingdon, Centre, Blair, and Mifflin Counties had forty-eight furnaces, forty-two forges, and eight rolling mills.

Williamsport became the greatest lumber producing city in the United States in the 1860's, with more than 300,000,000 feet of lumber passing through its log boom in some years. For nearly two decades, in the 1870's

BUILDING A CHARCOAL MOUND

The men shown in this picture are on Snowy Mountain in Franklin County. They are piling small logs so as to form a mound. Note the notched log that is used as a stair to reach the top of the mound. After a mound was built, most of it was covered with ground so that the logs would char rather than be consumed by the fire.

and 1880's, the West Branch Valley of the Susquehanna produced more board feet of lumber than any other region of similar size in the world.

During much of the last half of the nineteenth century, Central Pennsylvania was one of the most important lumber-producing centers on the entire globe. In order to recapture the precise facts, the lore, and the spirit of that era, the Pennsylvania Historical and Museum Commission erected the Pennsylvania Lumber Museum in Potter County, adjacent to the Denton Hill State Park. The Museum was opened in 1972. It is filled with exhibits of tools and equipment used in Central Pennsylvania lumbering a century ago.

Beside the main building of the Museum there is a full-scale logging camp with blacksmith shop and a "stemwinder" logging locomotive.

An annual Woodsmen's Carnival is held at the Lumber Museum. At the Carnival held on the week-end of August 3, 4 and 5, 1973, a blacksmith and other craftsmen performed tasks of the kind that were performed in Central Pennsylvania logging camps of the 1880's and 1890's. More than 2,700 visitors came to the Museum on August 4. On that date an orientation program was repeated at least twenty-seven times, each time to a "full house."

CRAFT DAYS AT THE PENNSYLVANIA LUMBER MUSEUM

The man in the foreground, seated, is operating a foot-pedal shaper typical of the 1890's. The "stemwinder" logging locomotive is seen in the background. The picture was taken in August 1973.

Main Building

Logging Camp

THE PENNSYLVANIA LUMBER MUSEUM

Built by the Pennsylvania Historical and Museum Commission, the Pennsylvania Lumber Museum houses many tools and much equipment used by lumbermen in Central Pennsylvania in the late 1800's. The Museum is located on U.S. Route 6, between Coudersport and Galeton, and is adjacent to Denton Hill State Park in Potter County. The cluster of buildings in bottom picture is typical of those that furnished sleeping space, kitchen, "dining hall," storeroom, blacksmith shop, and other necessary facilities for a large lumbering operation.

END VIEW OF THE LOGGING CAMP AT THE LUMBER MUSEUM
In this replica of a Central Pennsylvania logging camp, we see in the foreground the loading dock and the stable. Next is the saw filer's shack, and next to it the combination blacksmith and carpenter shop, and then, in background, the building housing the kitchen and "dining hall" on the first floor and the sleeping quarters on the second floor.

In the latter half of the 19th century lumbering operations moved farther and farther into the mountains. Men cut the large white pines and other timber trees and hauled the logs to splash dams or to sawmills, or to large streams on which the logs could be rafted to mill or market. Hemlock trees were cut for their bark. The bark was peeled on the mountainside and hauled to tanneries where hides were converted into leather through the use of the tannic acid in the hemlock bark. Tanneries in Central Pennsylvania tanned millions of hides with the acid from the bark of hemlock trees on the nearby mountains. Paper manufacturing and the wood chemical industry came to Central Pennsylvania because of its extensive forests. Paper mills such as those found in Lock Haven, Tyrone, and Williamsburg required enormous quantities of pulpwood from softwood trees such as aspen, hemlock, pine, and spruce. Men living back in the mountains cut and hauled pulpwood for the mills until nearly all of the pulpwood was imported from Canada, Sweden, and other distant places.

"SNAKING" (SKIDDING) A STRING OF LOGS

When trees were felled they were cut into saw logs and then pulled to a nearby log pile, from which they were loaded on sleds in winter and on wagons during the remainder of the year and hauled to a sawmill, or to a large stream for floating to a mill or to a river "port" where lumber merchants gathered to purchase logs. On a small lumbering operation the logs were "snaked" to the mill.

SLEDDING LOGS TO THE MILL

A typical winter operation in the mountains of Central Pennsylvania from about 1880 to about 1910.

LOGS WERE MOVED TO THE MILL BY HORSES AND BY LOCOMOTIVES

A team of horses was used to skid the logs from the stump to a railroad built deep into the forest late in the 19th century and early in the 20th. A train of cars gathered the logs that were brought to the tracks. The train then hauled the logs to the sawmill, thus developing lumbering into a massive activity in the heart of the forest. The team and the locomotive shown here were photographed at the Pennsylvania Lumber Museum in 1973.

TANNERY AT COSTELLO, POTTER COUNTY

Built by P. H. Costello & Company in 1881. The Costellos bought a tract of timber, approximately 4,000 acres, on the Sinnemahoning. Their tannery made sole leather but no other product. Their tannery was for a time reputed to be the largest in the world. This picture is from a photograph taken on May 8, 1918. The abandoned buildings were still standing in 1936.

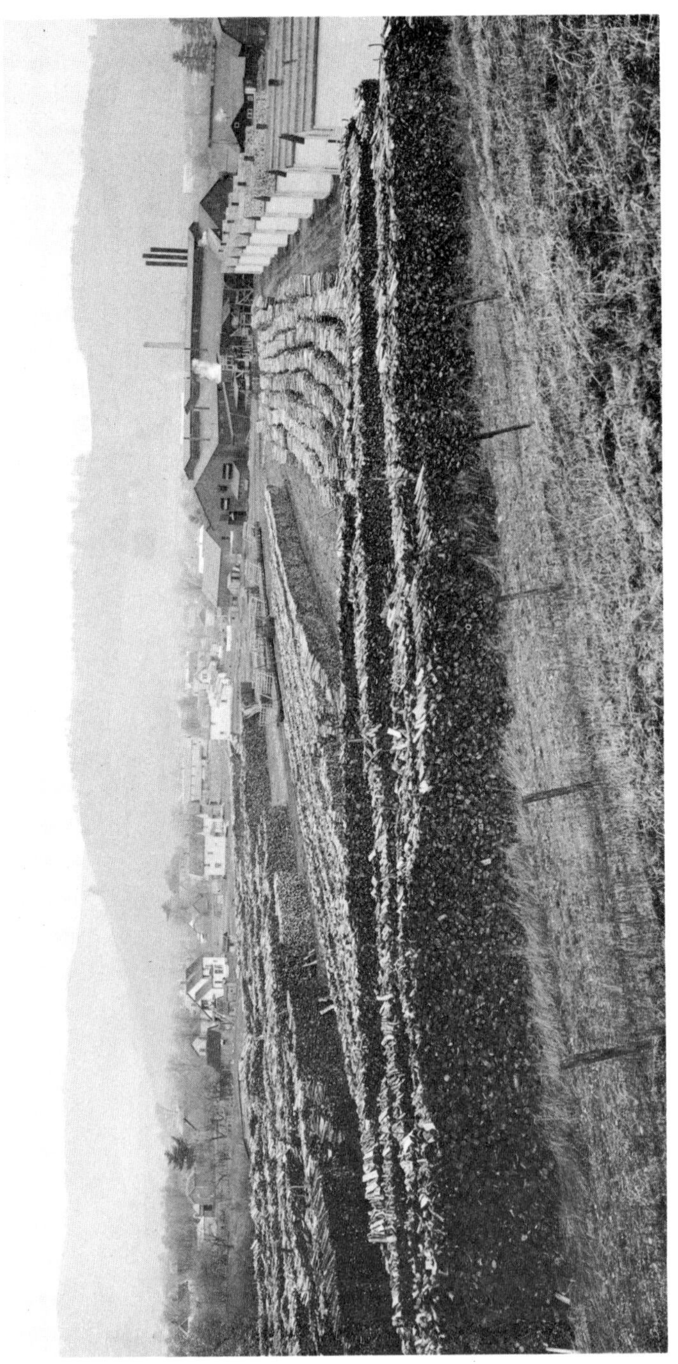

THE WOOD CHEMICAL INDUSTRY GAVE EMPLOYMENT TO MOUNTAIN FOLKS

Soon after the Civil War, chemistry aided the introduction of many new products. The manufacture of wood alcohol and related items, especially for industrial purposes, became a large operation in the wooded Allegheny Plateau. A wood chemical plant required an almost endless stream of logs. This picture shows the plant of the Gray Chemical Company at Roulette in Potter County. From a photograph taken in 1870.

The coming of the Pennsylvania Canal, the Allegheny Portage Railroad, and the Pennsylvania Railroad transformed parts of Perry, Juniata, Mifflin, Huntingdon, and Blair Counties into a prosperous agricultural and industrial area. Similarly, the construction of the West Branch Canal and the Sunbury and Erie Railroad (later known as the Philadelphia and Erie and then as the Pennsylvania Railroad) converted much of Lycoming and Clinton Counties into a bustling farming and manufacturing area.

By the early 1880's mountainous parts of Central and Northwestern Pennsylvania were being penetrated on a large scale by lumbermen, and Pennsylvania became the greatest lumber producing State in the Union. After the timber was cut, families moved in and established farms on the flattest and least stony parts of the mountaintops, as in the high land immediately east of Lock Haven where the Bald Eagle Mountain attains a width of approximately twelve miles, from Pine Station on the River to Loganton in Sugar Valley. This section of the Bald Eagle has been known locally as "Pine Mountain."

AN INCLINED PLANE ON THE ALLEGHENY PORTAGE RAILROAD

In the 1830's and 1840's the Allegheny Portage Railroad, extending from Hollidaysburg in Blair County to Johnstown in Cambria County, was an engineering wonder. By means of a series of ten inclined planes it carried canal boats and railroad cars over the main stem of the Allegheny Mountains. Thus it made possible a system of transportation between Philadelphia and Pittsburgh that was much more satisfactory than stagecoaching and Conestoga wagon freighting. This picture shows the top of one of the inclined planes. A stationary steam engine pulled the boats and cars up the incline by means of a cable.

HORSESHOE CURVE

Opened to traffic on February 15, 1854, the Horseshoe Curve is the Pennsylvania Railroad's most famous landmark and for more than a century has been considered an engineering wonder. Its curved grade up an exceedingly difficult face of the Alleghenies enabled the Pennsylvania Railroad Company to acquire a relatively direct route from Philadelphia to Pittsburgh. Nevertheless, the wisdom of selecting such an unfavorable place to cross the Alleghenies has frequently been questioned.

Some of those people who moved to the mountaintops in Central Pennsylvania wanted to escape the regimentation of society, some moved there in order to acquire land of their own, some out of a sense of adventure, and some to live peacefully in the midst of nature. Some who wanted a farm of their own could not afford to buy a valley farm but could afford to purchase mountain land.

The soil on those mountaintop farms was thin. The growing season was short because of frost late in spring and early in autumn. The farming was arduous, more so than in the valleys where the soil and climate were less hostile and where markets were at hand. The mountain families were equal to the situation. They built houses and barns, planted orchards, and tilled the land. Being largely isolated from the "valley people" they developed a camaraderie among themselves. Living close to nature and far from encyclopedias and the latest conveniences, they nourished the folktales that they heard, and created a repertoire of their own. Some of those tales were original and some undoubtedly were local adaptations of folktales that had been repeated in Europe for several centuries and brought to America.

III

A Mountain Community In The Early 1930's

In that part of Clinton County where the Bald Eagle Mountain attains a width of approximately twelve miles, from Pine Station on the West Branch of the Susquehanna River to Loganton in Sugar Valley, there was an isolated community in the early 1930's. That community on top of the Bald Eagle Mountain had its cemetery, abandoned Lutheran church (Mount Zion), a one-room school then still in use, a bottomless road (the Pine-Loganton Road), abandoned and overgrown lumber roads, and no electric or telephone service. There was no postal service except at a row of rural mail boxes adjacent to Mount Zion Church and at other mail boxes along the road from there to Loganton, and at the post office in Pine Station and in Loganton. Sam Frankenburger was the first mailman on the mountain. Luther Best was the second, and he brought the mail in 1932. In winter the mail was carried in a covered sleigh and frequently the mailman drove through the windswept fields to avoid huge snow drifts in the road. On the side of the sleigh there was a sign "U. S. Mail."

When standing on the bank of the West Branch of the Susquehanna River, at or near the village of Pine Station, and looking at the Bald Eagle Mountain, one part of its north wall, Old Round Top, commands attention. In May 1973 Mrs. Mary Sour Gardner of Pine Station wrote the following poem about Old Round Top.

From my home along the river
Here in the village of Pine
I can see the line of mountains
That make a picture very fine.

I can see three mountains to the east
And three more by looking west
But when I look straight ahead
I can see Old Round Top best.

When I was just a little tot
Old Round Top seemed so very high,
I thought if I could climb to its top
I'd be able to reach to the sky.

THE NORTH SIDE OF THE BALD EAGLE MOUNTAIN AT PINE STATION, CLINTON COUNTY

From a photograph taken in 1974 near the town of Avis. Old Round Top is shown in the center. High tableland behind Old Round Top was the scene of extensive lumbering in the 1880's and 1890's, and the home of many mountain folks from the 1880's to 1935, and of a smaller number in 1974.

Families have never lived on its slopes
Not as far as I have known
But hunters go there with high, high hopes
For its truly a hunter's zone.

Old Round Top is a landmark
To each one who can recall
Its shape and natural beauty
Winter, summer, spring or fall.

No matter where you've traveled
Or where you choose to roam,
When you can see Old Round Top
You know you're almost home.

There were farms surrounded by forest in that isolated area on top of the mountain, and immediately south of Old Round Top. Some farms were separated from each other by more than a mile of woods. When a farm was deserted the forest began to "move in." As a result, in 1935 one could find here and there on the top of the mountain the foundations of a house and a few old apple trees near it. The fields, orchard, and site of the house were already hidden in a thick growth of young trees. Each of those deserted farms had its own story. In 1932 one of them, on the west side of the Pine-Loganton Road and approximately a mile north of Mount Zion Church, consisted of only three fields, a few old apple trees, and the cellar

MOUNT ZION CHURCH AS IT LOOKED IN 1932
All six of the Rich children were baptized in this church.

walls of the house. It was the farm of James L. O'Donnell and his wife. In addition to cultivating the soil, Mr. O'Donnell also operated a stave mill on Spring Creek, at the edge of the farm. He made barrel staves, round heads for nail kegs, and wood shingles. The O'Donnell house burned in 1903. Mr. and Mrs. O'Donnell moved to Pine Station and operated the Pine Station Hotel for a number of years.

The O'Donnells were a connecting link between the families who settled on the top of the Bald Eagle Mountain in Wayne, Crawford, Greene, and Lamar Townships, Clinton County, almost as soon as the timber was first being removed on a large scale, and the families who lived there in the early 1930's.

One can visualize the mountaintop community in its earliest days by consulting D. S. Maynard's 1875 book entitled *Historical View of Clinton County, From Its Earliest Settlement To The Present Time*. The book includes a chapter on each of the four townships in which the community was located. In writing about Wayne Township, Maynard stated:

> About two-thirds of the surface of the township is elevated several hundred feet above the river . . . .
>
> The soil of the highlands of the township is generally sandy, and in some places contains shale. It is as a general thing susceptible of cultivation. (Page 218).

MR. JAMES L. O'DONNELL AND MELVINA, HIS WIFE

The O'Donnells farmed on the top of Bald Eagle Mountain, in Wayne Township, Clinton County, until 1903. After moving into the Pine Station Hotel in that year they operated the hotel until it burned in 1923. They spent their last years at the foot of the mountain, near Pine Station. Mr. O'Donnell was born in 1852 and died in 1942.

Maynard said, except for Nippenose Valley, nearly all of Crawford Township "is mostly unimproved and unsettled." (Page 144). Lumbering had already become an important activity in the highlands of Greene Township by 1875. Maynard commented:

> The timber of the entire township orginally consisted of heavy growths of pine, oak, chestnut, maple, &c.; the elevated portions still afford a large amount of choice varieties, which each season is being reduced by the operations of lumbermen. (Page 160).
>
> ° ° °
>
> The mountain portion of the township was not settled till quite a number of years after the valley. Among the first to penetrate the highland wilds and make permanent improvements, was Jacob Frantz, who constructed a saw mill upon the head waters of McElhattan Run, about 1830 or '35. After the death of Frantz the property passed through the hands of several different owners. Among others, J. R. Fredericks, now of Pine Station, and A. T. Nichols, of Williamsport. At present the entire

tract owned by Frantz, which contained seven or eight hundred acres, and about a thousand acres additional is owned by Jamison & Co., and is under the management of Mr. Andrew Jamison, one of the firm. The original mill, which of course was run by water, has been replaced by a good substantial structure, with steam power attached.

A mile or so below Jamison's mill, on the same stream, J. Herman has a saw mill, and on Long Run, near the northwest corner of the township is what is called the "Phildadelphia mill." It was built by Thomas Furst about the year 1845. A post-office called "Rosecrans," has been established at this mill, it being located on the stage route from Lock Haven to Logansville. [Now, 1974, called Loganton].

Hoffa's mill is located near the northeast corner of the township, on a tributary of Fishing Creek. It is now in operation. The other principal mills are: Murray's, at Carroll; and Kemerer's, located about one mile and a-half northwest of Logansville.

After the first settlement was made upon the mountain lands of Greene township, it was not long before they were "taken up" by hardy and industrious Germans, from the neighboring counties, and the result is: today there are many as finely cultivated and highly productive farms on what is called Sugar Valley Mountain, as there are in any other part of the county, and more; the general improvements, such as roads, fences, buildings, etc., compare favorably with those of localities that have been settled much longer. Upon the "mountain" there are already several school houses and three churches; the latter are called respectively, "Mount Pleasant church," "Mount Zion church," and "Green Grove Chapel." The following are the names of some of the prominent settlers of the mountain lands: J. Schitze, M. G. Wismer, P. Wert, J. Herman on the western end, and F. Stark, lamp-black manufacturer, J. Henninger, J. Bickster, and J. Ambig, on the east end. (Pages 163-164).

Between the O'Donnell farm and Pine Station the Ramms (George Ramm & Company) had a sawmill at the time Maynard's history of Clinton County was published in 1875. That mill provided employment to people who worked at the mill and to men who hauled logs down the mountain to the mill and to others who hauled the sawed lumber from the mill. The Ramm sawmill, a reminder of the years when lumbering was big business on the Bald Eagle Mountain, was located part way up the north side of the mountain, on Henry Run, about a mile and three-quarters from Pine Station and approximately three miles from the O'Donnell farm. In 1974 the foundations of two buildings can be seen at the mill site.

Logs destined for the Ramm sawmill that were hauled down the mountain by teamsters were unloaded at the "rollway." The logs were pushed over the brink. They slid down the steep bank to the millpond on Henry Run. The mill was operated by waterpower. When the water was low in Henry Run the mill was powered by a steam engine. A large bull wheel pulled the logs up to the mill for sawing while still wet. The Ramm accounts kept at the Sour Ferry show that the Ramms were making many trips across the river at Pine Station with wagons and two horses in November and December 1863, and in January, February, and March, 1864, and on through the years. In 1881, on June 23, they made nine trips across the river, and the next month, on July 5, eighteen trips, each time with two horses. Their mill finally burned, perhaps in early May, 1893, as the last entry in the Ramm accounts kept at the Sour Ferry is dated May 8 of that year. The accounts are preserved by Mrs. Mary Sour Gardner of Pine Station.

THE SOUR FERRY AT NORTH END OF PINE-LOGANTON ROAD

This ferry was in existence 1814-1918 and made it possible for the folks on the top of the Bald Eagle Mountain, and the people in the West Branch Valley, to cross the river conveniently, even with loaded wagons. From a photograph taken during the last years that the ferry was operating.

At the time the O'Donnells lived on top of the mountain the wagon traffic on the Pine-Loganton Road was heavy. There were "turnouts" so that a teamster with an empty wagon could pull to the side to let a teamster with a heavy load of logs pass. Teamsters with a heavy load signalled their approach by blowing horns as they came down the mountain.

MICHAEL N. SOUR, SURVEYOR OF THE PINE-LOGANTON ROAD

A court order was given in 1847 for the sawing and laying of the road. Sour was Deputy Surveyor of Clinton County and the Commissioners' Clerk. He surveyed the road, starting at the Sour Ferry on the West Branch and proceeding to Loganville, as the Sugar Valley town was then known. Sour's descendant, Mrs. Mary Sour Gardner of Pine Station, presented to the Clinton County Historical Society in 1967 the survey map that Michael N. Sour made of the Pine-Loganton Road.

LOGANTON, THE "METROPOLIS" OF SUGAR VALLEY

From an aerial photograph taken in or about 1950, Loganton had a population of 385 in 1890; 432 in 1900; 375 in 1910; 254 in 1920; 264 in 1930; 385 in 1960; and 436 in 1970. Chief town in Sugar Valley, it has remained as a stable and almost static community for nearly a century. The Keystone Shortway, Interstate Highway 80, now passes within a mile of Loganton and is transforming the town and its valley.

The accompanying map shows the top of the Bald Eagle Mountain in Wayne, Crawford, Greene, and Lamar Townships, Clinton County, and the location of roads and buildings of the mountain community. The map is reproduced from a section of the United States Geological Survey quadrangle, "Lock Haven," 1923 edition.

The families in the Clinton County community on top of the Bald Eagle Mountain raised most of their own food and sold vegetables, eggs, poultry, beef, pork, and other products from their farms at curb market in Lock Haven, the county seat.

In the early 1930's the farmers placed a bell on each cow and in the morning turned the cows out to browse all day and kept them in the barn at night. The Roy G. Rich family enclosed a tract of about five acres of pasture and approximately forty-five acres of woods, with three strands of barbed wire. The cows stayed in the woods during the hot part of summer days. In the woods they found small clumps of grass and tender shoots on brush.

THE RICH FAMILY IN 1930

Mr. Roy G. Rich at edge of picture; Mrs. Rich holding their youngest child, Franklin; Glen and Ethel in the background; Alvina in foreground; Warren and Evelyn in front of Mrs. Rich.

SUSQUEHANNA
RIVER
CENTRAL
NEW YORK
PENNSYLVANIA
BM 566
BM 561
541
Browns
Pine Station
McElhattan
Wayne School No 2
603
Youngdale
689
Shoemaker Park
W A Y N E M O U N T A I N
G L E N
Lock Haven Reservoir
East Kammerdiner Run
Spring Run
Creek
Chestnut Flat
1720
1335
1446
997
1655
1851
1585
1710
Mt Zion Church
1792
1743
NIPPENO
VALLE
Red Sc
N A W F O R D
1727
1563
Spruce Run
1681
1693
1677
1248
1665
1693
Rosecrans
1711
1740
Rianzares Mtn
2293
Pepper Run
Hopple Hollow
SUGAR VALLEY
G R E E N
1562
Sulphur
1280
Royer School
Loganton
BM 1297
1663

A few years earlier, before the chestnut blight began to strike the community about 1918, pigs were turned loose to roam in chestnut groves to eat chestnuts. The pigs returned to their trough late in the day to receive supplemental feed.

The people on the mountain gathered chestnuts, ate them raw, boiled them, and roasted them. One large area, Chestnut Flat, three miles west of Mount Zion Church, was covered with large chestnut trees. Almost anywhere on the top of the mountain there were beautiful chestnut trees until the blight wiped them out. Approximately one-tenth of the trees on the top of the mountain were chestnut until time of the blight.

In the early 1930's peaches, plums, apples, pears, and cherries were raised on those mountain farms but none of the fruit trees were sprayed. The fruit was reasonably good. In 1918 the fruit raised on those mountain farms, without any spraying, was very good. In 1974 it is almost impossible to raise edible fruit on the top of the Bald Eagle Mountain without spraying.

The people on the mountain obtained wood from the forest to heat their houses.

Through thrift and ingenuity they managed to get along with relatively little dependence upon the remainder of the world. Immediately before the Great Depression of the 1930's the men in that mountain community had an opportunity to supplement their income by cutting ties for the Pennsylvania Railroad, which passes through Pine Station, and by cutting pulpwood, by working in small sawmills scattered through the timberland, and by working for the State forestry department.

The people on the mountain made use of the resources at hand. Huckleberry picking was one of their summertime activities. In July of each year, often starting on July 4, they picked large quantities of wild huckleberries, a delicacy that compared favorably with the largest and best of present-day cultivated blue berries. The wild huckleberries were sweeter than the cultivated blue berries of today.

The large patches of huckleberries were found in areas that had been destroyed by forest fires several years previously. The berry crop was good the second year after a fire and continued to yield a good crop for several years, until the brush began to crowd the huckleberry bushes. During the 1920's and early 1930's forest fires were more of a menace in the United States than they have been since that time, because of the gradual improvement in the prevention, detection, and fighting of fires on timber and brush lands.

In the burned areas on the top of the Bald Eagle Mountain in Clinton County, and elsewhere in the mountains of Central Pennsylvania, the huckleberry bushes grew so densely, particularly at the higher elevations, that one pushed his way through the waste-high bushes. Some of the patches with the quantities of huckleberries were the most difficult to reach, in high, rocky places. In some patches the huckleberry bushes grew to a height of approximately eight feet and were referred to as "tree" huckleberries. Some huckleberry patches covered several acres, but the patches of tree huckleberries were much smaller, perhaps never more than an acre in extent. The tree huckleberries were found in swampy places.

Families on the top of Bald Eagle Mountain in the early 1930's would start out at about six o'clock in the morning to pick huckleberries and would carry their lunch. They took with them buckets and bushel baskets or other containers of about a bushel in size in which to put the berries they would pick.

Huckleberry picking was a dangerous operation. There were rattlesnakes and copperheads in the berry patches. They were on the ground, under the bushes and between the stones, waiting to devour rabbits that came to feed on the berries. The mountain folks were not particularly afraid of the deadly rattlesnake and the almost equally poisonous copperhead snake, but the mountain folks were cautious. A rattler and a copperhead will strike at a person, feeling instinctively that the person is about to attack them. Both have a tendency to move away when people approach, but sometimes they remain motionless. Rattlers do not always give their warning. Then, if a person places a bare hand, or a foot or leg not heavily protected, near the snake, not being aware of the snake's presence, there is real danger. Consequently, the huckleberry pickers approached a patch warily and pushed the bushes aside in front of them, sometimes with a long stick, looking for snakes to see if the immediate area was "safe." The parents kept the smaller children close as a means of protection, but left the very young children at home. Each of the berry pickers moved cautiously through the bushes during the day, watching where they stepped and where they reached with their hands.

The mountain folks knew, of course, that copperheads exude an odor like that of freshly sliced cucumbers. As a means of protecting themselves, the pickers were alert for the presence of that odor when moving about in a huckleberry patch. Some of the pickers who believed that the smell of onions was offensive to snakes, and drove them away, placed onion slices inside their socks or stockings before entering the patches.

Typically, the parents and the older children each carried an eight or ten quart bucket. The smaller children carried pails of the size they could handle. Each member of the family scooped the berries from the bushes into their buckets, with their hands. Some of the men and women were exceedingly adept at pulling a handful of berries at a time, clean, with scarcely any twigs or leaves. When a good patch was found the buckets were filled in an amazingly short time. They were emptied into the large baskets, and the picking continued until about six o'clock in the afternoon, but sometimes until dark, except at lunch time. It was not unusual for a family to return home in the evening with 100 quarts of berries. Some of the berries were sold at farmers' curb market in Lock Haven and the remainder were preserved in glass one-quart jars, to be made into pies all during the next winter.

Not only did the people on the top of the mountain in the early 1930's enjoy their folktales, they also delighted in telling stories about Sam Motter who was born in 1850 and had lived among them until his death in 1921. He had the best farmland on the mountain but spent much of his time in the forest. It seems that he caught those destructive wild animals, such as wildcats, on which the Commonwealth of Pennsylvania paid a bounty. Sam was an untamed, rugged individualist, and cared little about the feelings of other people, including his own family. He traveled in the woods without getting lost. He broke branches in a certain way as he walked through dense stands of timber or thick brush and thus found his way home. His son Arthur was his only son who could find him in the forest, and no doubt the only person who could find him.

It is said that Sam Motter was walking through the woods one night near Booneville in Sugar Valley and blundered into a large log pen built to catch a bear alive. Sam found himself imprisoned, with a live bear. The bear resented the intrusion and rushed at Sam. In his hand Sam had a steel trap for small game. He rebuked the bear with that small trap. Tradition has it that in the morning the man who hoped to catch a bear in the log pen found Sam Motter sleeping peacefully in one corner of the enclosure and the bear crouched in the other, wimpering like a child.

Even though being king of the forest, Sam Motter was not always able to maintain the most amicable relationships with his neighbors. Several men entered his house one time, intending to treat him violently. There was a small door in the wall of the house, through which firewood was pushed in from outdoors. When the irate men entered one part of Sam's house he quickly slipped through the "wood hole" in another part of the house and disappeared into the woods.

Sam Motter seldom wore shoes, saying they hurt his feet. Learning that he had inherited a fortune from his father (probably $2,500.00) and that he had to go to California to get it, he *walked* from his mountain farm, *barefooted*, across the United States, to claim the legacy. Colonel Henry Wharton Shoemaker wrote a sketch of Motter. It was published in the form of a pamphlet entitled *California Sam*. The following poem about Motter was written in 1973 by Mary Sour Gardner of Pine Station.

SAM MOTTER AND THREE OF HIS CHILDREN

The boy standing is Arthur Motter. The other two children have not been identified. Sam had five daughters and six sons: Tillie, Dora, Laura, Lulu, Florence, Arthur, Harry, Charles, Norris, Jess, and David. This picture is from a tintype owned by Mrs. Esther Motter Swinter, daughter of Arthur Motter and granddaughter of Sam Motter.

SAM

Many winters and summers ago
A mountain man we used to know
Claimed he walked barefoot in the snow
He could crack chestnut burrs with his bare heels
Just think how prickly a chesnut burr feels
His name was Motter, that's all I knew
Except that he seldom wore a shoe.
His home was back on the mountain wild
This impressed me as a very small child
He was a strong and hardy man
And all my folks just called him 'Sam.'

Sam Motter is buried in Mt. Pleasant Cemetery at Rosecrans, a small village in Greene Township on top of the Bald Eagle Mountain. The cemetery is within three miles of the Motter farm.

In 1948 Mr. and Mrs. Roy G. Rich bought the 229-acre Motter Place, about a mile from the farm on which they lived. They moved to the Motter Place and lived there much of the time during the remainder of Mr. Rich's life, although in later years spending part of the year in the valley, near Pine Station. At the Motter Place they were "snowed in" frequently for weeks at a time.

MR. AND MRS. ROY G. RICH AT THE MOTTER PLACE

From a photograph taken in March 1960 when the mountaintop was covered with thirty-seven inches of snow. The Riches stocked up with food at the beginning of each winter and survived excellently.

Among Mr. and Mrs. Rich's interesting experiences at the Motter Place were somewhat frequent visits by bear who were insistent upon tearing slats off the corncrib and having a banquet. For three summers the Riches could not keep slats on their corncrib. A bear tore slats off and carried corn away. Slats were replaced. A bear returned and helped himself to corn. The slats were nailed on again, and so on. For a time the visitor was a long-legged, rangy, unkempt looking animal, known locally as a "dog bear." At other times the intruder was short-legged, sleek, and rather aristocratic looking and was known locally as a "hog bear." The bear came to the corncrib at night, and sometimes were bold enough to come during the daylight hours.

The City of Lock Haven bought the mountaintop farm on which Mr. and Mrs. Rich and their children lived for many years, before Mr. and Mrs. Rich purchased the Motter Place. The City made the purchase in order to extend its control over the watershed from which the City obtains its water supply. The house and barn on the farm on which the Roy G. Rich family lived and labored in their earlier years have been removed and the forest is reseeding rapidly that former clearing in the wilderness, just as it reseeded hundreds of former mountain farms throughout much of Central Pennsylvania.

As in other communities, there was a shiftless family. Most members of that family seldom supported themselves. Some of them were entertaining conversationalists but seldom worked today or prepared for tomorrow. They lived in squalor. Some of the men had a taste for alcohol. Prior to public welfare on a large scale in 1933, firewood and food were delivered to their door at the expense of the township. At various periods the children did not attend school, but in other years some of them did. Fortunately, several members of the family, in at least two generations, were industrious and respectable persons.

The people on the Bald Eagle Mountain had numerous interesting experiences. A Mrs. Sarah Jane Confer, widow of Jonathan Confer, who lived on the Pine-Loganton Road walked nine miles along that road, over the top of the mountain and down to Pine Station to see her daughter Lydia (Mrs. George Troutman), carrying a bucket of milk. When she arrived at Pine Station she found that the milk had turned to butter!

From the 1880's to 1935 the chief places of contact with the outside world for the folks on the top of the Bald Eagle Mountain in Clinton County were Loganton, Pine Station, and Lock Haven. Loganton was a farming community. Pine Station was a bustling place because of the railroad, lumbering, a pumping station on an oil pipeline, and the Camp Meetings of the Evangelical Association. Lock Haven has been the county seat since formation of Clinton as an independent county in 1839. It was a rather important railroad junction point and the home of a State normal school which became a State teachers college and then a State college. Lock Haven also became a manufacturing center, with two large paper mills, one founded in 1883, the other in 1919, consuming pulpwood cut on the Bald Eagle Mountain.

In the early 1930's the Roy G. Rich family, the Weavers, the Sheasleys, the Eyers, the Jamesons, the Lehmans, the Shaffers, the Royers, and a few other families comprised the total population of the community on the top of the Bald Eagle Mountain. The following pictures reproduced from photographs taken between 1918 and 1974, and accompanying text, focus on that community. It was in that community and at the foot of the mountain, at Pine Station, that the folktales included in this book were told and retold for several generations.

MOUNT ZION SCHOOL AND CEMETERY, SPRING 1973

Cornerstone of Mount Zion Church in foreground, midway between school and opposite edge of picture. The Church was torn down in June 1962.

TEACHER AND PUPILS AT MOUNT ZION SCHOOL IN OR ABOUT 1924

The woodland scene used as a background was found just outside the schoolhouse door. The families represented in this picture are Weaver, Rich, Eyer, Bixel, and Miller. Elva Lehman, in long white dress, was the teacher of the group.

GLEN RICH AND HIS SISTER ALVINA IN THEIR YARD, WITH "DAISY"

From a photograph taken in or about 1932. The ridge to the southwest of the Rich farm is shown in the background. On the side of that ridge, and approximately a mile from Riches, were the remains of the Bickford Place, an abandoned farm. In 1932 its fields were being threatened by the forest and its windowless farmhouse ***was deteriorating rapidly.***

MOUNTAIN FARM SCENE

MR. HENRY EYER AND MYRTLE, HIS WIFE

From a photoghaph taken about 1935. Mr. Eyer and his son Alvin farmed approximately thirty acres. Through sheer persistence they turned their part of the mountaintop into a garden spot. Mr. Henry eyer was born in 1876 and died in 1958.

MR. JAMES SHEASLEY AND HIS SISTER, MRS. ELMER WEAVER

From a photograph taken at James Sheasley's house about 1935. James Sheasley lived on the Pine-Loganton Road about two hundred yards south of the Weaver Place.

MR. ELMER WEAVER AND HIS DAUGHTER HELEN

From a photograph taken about 1935 at the Weaver Place, adjacent to Mount Zion Church. "Paw" Weaver as he was known on the mountain spent much of his life taking care of his team of horses and hauling saw logs that had been cut from trees felled on the mountain, and taking care of his small farm. In his later years, after 1935, he worked with a road maintenance crew several miles from his home. Mr. Weaver was born in 1868 and died in 1955.

THE MOTTER PLACE AS IT LOOKED IN OR ABOUT 1918

Most of its 229 acres are nearly level. Those acres were the home of Sam Motter, a fearless person about whom it has frequently been said that he captured a wildcat with his bare hands.

THE OVERDORF FAMILY AT THEIR MOUNTAIN HOME, FORMERLY KNOWN AS THE MOTTER PLACE

From a photograph taken in 1918, showing Raymond Overdorf, Fronie, his wife, on the horse, his mother, and his small brother, Russell. Sam Motter, almost indistinguishable, is on the porch.

THE BRUNGARD-JAMESON-WEBER HOUSE, 1974

Located approximately three-fourth of a mile from Mount Zion School. This house was the birthplace of D. M. Brungard, County Superintendent of Schools in Clinton County in the late 19th century. In the early 1930's the Christie Jameson family lived here. The place was purchased by Dr. and Mrs. Harry F. Weber in 1937. The Webers soon discovered hand-hewn logs under the siding and they restored the house to its original beauty. Rather than farm their fifty mountaintop acres, the Webers planted evergreen trees in their fields, now a beautiful stand of timber.

LOCK HAVEN AS IT LOOKED IN OR ABOUT 1900

From a photograph in the collections of the Pennsylvania Historical and Museum Commission, and formerly in the collections of the Commercial Museum, Philadelphia. In the heyday of lumbering in Clinton County, Lock Haven was already an important town, and a place where the mountain folks could sell their farm produce and where they could purchase almost anything they needed.

Festival and Fair

OX-ROAST

AT

Pine Station, Pa.

JULY 4, 1908

PROGRAM

Greased Pig Catch. Wheel Barrow Mate. Sack Race. Potato Race for the Ladies. Candle Race for the Ladies. Bicycle Race. Lean Man's Running Race. Fat Man's Running Race. Tub Race on the River. Base Ball Games. Dancing Afternoon and Evening on the Platform, Music furnished by an Orchestra. There will be Speakers from all Parts.

Prizes will be given in all Contests.
An All-Day Shooting Match will be held.
We guarantee a good day's Outing for all.
Music furnished by the Avis Band.

CHICKEN AND WAFFLE DINNER AND SUPPER

For Benefit of Church

Fireworks in the Evening

FROM THE 1880's TO 1935 THE MOUNTAIN FOLKS WENT DOWN THE MOUNTAIN TO PINE STATION TO PARTICIPATE IN VARIOUS EVENTS

A GATHERING ON THE CAMP GROUND AT FOOT OF OLD ROUND TOP IN OR ABOUT 1908

From a postcard picture of the Quiggle—Montgomery Reunion. The group is seated on the tabernacle benches, facing the pavilion, with some persons standing in back. The Camp Ground drew enormous crowds for years, from 1871. Undoubtedly the folks on the top of the Bald Eagle Mountain frequently walked or drove down the mountain to the Camp Ground for it was a great attraction. A sketch concerning formation, growth and activities of "The Pine Station Camp-Meeting Association" is given on pages 236-238 of my book, "Adventures and Philosophy of a Pennsylvania Dutchman."

IV

The Lore of Central Pennsylvania

The Keystone State is rich in both lore and history. George Korson's book, *Pennsylvania Songs and Legends*, published by the University of Pennsylvania Press in 1949, comprises a large sampling of the lore of Pennsylvania. The lore of the mountain folks and of the valley people in the middle third of the State consists of their traditions, customs, and oral tales, rhymes, and sayings—in other words their folkways. As used in this book, the term lore refers to "traditional knowledge" rather than to precise, scientific facts. As used here, lore relates to the entire field of folklore, but to nothing else. Historical events and trends are mentioned as a framework in which the lore developed. The lore discussed in this book refers mainly to the traditional knowledge of a particular group of people, the mountain folks of Central Pennsylvania. The book includes fascinating fragments of their folkways and of their folktales.

The lore of Central Pennsylvania includes folk songs, folktales, the use of herbs in the healing of the sick, and superstitious beliefs handed down orally from one generation to the next. These in composite, for any rather homogeneous group of people, are usually referred to as folklore.

As in some other parts of the United States, a body of tradition and custom was created in Central Pennsylvania as a result of experience in clearing the land, warding off the wild beasts, and preparing to meet raids by the Indians, and through the effect of such developments as the Revolutionary War, the establishment of churches, and a democratic form of government, schools, the manufacture of iron in charcoal furnaces, the building of canals and railroads, the rise of lumbering and tanning, the expansion of agriculture and the mushrooming of many kinds of manufacturing establishments. The lore of Central Pennsylvania is as broad as the experiences of its inhabitants.

In addition, lore, in the form of poems and legends, grew up around geographical features such as the Susquehanna and Juniata Rivers, Chimney Rocks near Hollidaysburg, and Shikellamy's Profile, a bare rock formation jutting from a high bluff opposite Sunbury and looking out over the Susquehanna River.

THE SUSQUEHANNA RIVER AT LIVERPOOL, PERRY COUNTY

From "American Scenery," a famous book by N. P. Willis, published in 1840 and reprinted in 1971. For more than a century and a half the beauty of Central Pennsylvania's Susquehanna and its surrounding mountains has been appreciated widely. Note the boats on the river and the boat on the canal. Events occurring in the Susquehanna Valley in the days of its canalboat traffic, approximately 1830-1889, produced songs and folktales.

In 1804 Alexander Wilson wrote a beautiful poem about the Susquehanna. Its opening lines are as follows:

Hail, charming river, pure transparent flood!
Unstained by noxious swamps or choking mud;
Thundering through broken rocks in whirling foam;
Or pleased o'er beach of glittering sand to roam;
Green be thy banks, sweet forest-wandering stream!

Bright Alfarata, a poem about an Indian girl and the Juniata River, was written in 1840 by Mrs. Marion Dix Sullivan. The poem begins with the following stanza:

Wild roved an Indian Girl,
Bright Alfarata
Where sweep the waters
Of the blue Juniata!
Swift as an antelope
Through the forest going,
Loose were her jetty locks,
In many tresses flowing.

Mrs. Sullivan was the daughter-in-law of the famous revolutionary general, John Sullivan. The song, known also as *The Blue Juniata*, was inspired by a trip on a canal packet boat up the Juniata River. For at least two decades it was one of the most popular songs and was widely known.

Chimney Rocks, in the Juniata Valley and south of Hollidaysburg, are formations in limestone that rise dramatically from their surroundings. These tall rocks have been a curiosity for generations. They are among the most interesting and scenic rock formations in Pennsylvania. In a sense they resemble formations in the Garden of the Gods near Colorado Springs, Colorado. Pennsylvania's Chimney Rocks have been owned by the Blair County Historical Society since December 14, 1923. On October 17, 1924, a bronze marker was placed on the Pulpit Rock of the Chimney Rocks in recognition of the gift of land to the Society and to designate the plot for public use.

Shikellamy's Profile, too, is an important part of the lore of Central Pennsylvania. Shikellamy, an Oneida, lived at present Sunbury as Vice-Regent of the Six Nations, and for them he had dominion over Central Pennsylvania. He was perhaps the most influential Indian in Pennsylvania in the eighteenth century and was a true friend of the white man.

On the end of the Blue Hill in Snyder County there is a profile in rock that resembles a human face, often said to resemble Chief Shikellamy. This point, across the Susquehanna from Sunbury, affords a grand view up and down the river. The end of the Blue Hill was also the site of John

CHIMNEY ROCKS, NEAR HOLLIDAYSBURG

These two tall, rugged chimneys, standing like sentinels, present an unusual spectacle. It is said that the Indians held council meetings here, that the fires of the Indians burned at this lookout, and that smoke signals were sent to warriors in the valley.

Mason's leaning tower, a lookout near the Shikellamy Profile. The tower was built in 1839 by the eccentric John Mason and was destroyed in 1864. The locality of the Profile and the tower was frequented by picnickers and sightseers during all of the last half of the nineteenth century. The following four lines about the Shikellamy Profile are from *Legends of the Susquehanna* by Truman H. Purdy.

Half up those rocks, conspicuous in place,
    Time's hand has chisell'd Shikellamy's face,
Which, looking eastward o'er the rippling wave,
    Beholds the place where chieftains made his grave.

Stage-coaching and wagon-freighting from Philadelphia to the Ohio Valley and beyond, and the stagecoach taverns along the principal nineteenth century roads through the middle third of the State, provided the basis for many tales, as did also the limestone caves and man's battle with storms, floods, and wild beasts, particularly wolves, wildcats, and panthers.

The Civil War and Confederate invasions, too, generated oft-repeated tales. The southern part of Central Pennsylvania was invaded by Confederate troops in 1862, in 1863, and in 1864. Confederate troops terrorized the inhabitants of Fulton, Franklin, Cumberland, Dauphin, and Adams Counties. Mercersburg and Chambersburg in Franklin County were raided in October 1862. The crucial engagement of the Civil War was fought at Gettysburg July 1-3, 1863. The next year, on July 30, 1864, the Confederates burned the town of Chambersburg.

Communal societies and engineering feats, too, provided a basis for lore, such as folktales. In the eastern half of McKean County the Teutonia settlement, established in 1841 by the Society of Industry, and the construction of the Kinzua Viaduct in 1882, attracted attention. Teutonia, with more than 400 families, flowered quickly in the wilderness as a communal group and withered just as rapidly. The society failed in three years. The Kinzua Viaduct, a railroad bridge, was proclaimed as recently as 1963 as being the second highest viaduct in North America. It probably has never been surpassed in *both* length and height by any bridge in the entire world. The bridge as built originally and as rebuilt in 1900 to accommodate heavier locomotives, is 2,053 feet long and rises 301 feet above Kinzua Creek.

Often the members of a sophisticated society are not aware of their own folklore but are intrigued by the folklore of groups of persons who seem to be vastly different from and much less sophisticated than themselves. The nineteenth century folklore of people in the mountains of Central Penn-

SHIKELLAMY'S PROFILE

This rock formation on the end of the Blue Hill, opposite Sunbury, has attracted much attention for more than a century and is a reminder of an Indian chief who was an important friend of the white man in early colonial times. Shikellamy died in 1748.

sylvania or in the small villages at the foot of the mountains is fascinating. It reveals man's struggle with nature and his adjustment to isolation before the time of the explosion of knowledge and the technological revolution of mid and late twentieth century. That type of folklore was still lingering among the mountain folks of Central Pennsylvania as late as 1935.

Mountain folklore is fragile. It has largely disappeared in Pennsylvania since the 1930's because of the movement of the mountain people to the valleys, the improvement of mountain roads, and the extension of telephone and electric lines to places that formerly were isolated.

By the early 1930's a large percent of the mountain farms in Central Pennsylvania, including many of those farms high on the Bald Eagle Mountain in Clinton County, had been abandoned, perhaps more than half of them. The mountain people who remained were still repeating the folktales, and with great delight. However, the isolation was being eroded and the folktales would soon fade. The automobile was invading the mountaintops. Those people would soon be spending much more time in the valleys. Today, only forty years later, those folktales which survived until 1935 seem almost incredible. They are a reminder of a fascinating era when lumbering entered secluded parts of Central Pennsylvania and marginal (subsistence) farming followed in its wake for approximately a half century.

V

Folktales

A considerable part of this volume consists of folktales told to me by the mountain people. Folktales are an important and an interesting part of folklore. Folktales have existed in primitive societies for centuries, perhaps from the time when man was first able to use language reasonably well. Compulsory education, enormous circulation of newspapers and magazines, and the outreach of radio and television have wiped out nearly all the kinds of isolation in which the folktales of the more primitive peoples thrived.

A folktale is anonymous, endures for generations, is often the common property of people in widely separated places, and is circulated by word of mouth. A folktale is usually a story told for entertainment. Some folktales are about real people, such as Baron Hieronymus Karl Friedrich Munchhausen, 1720-1797, a German soldier, and "Davy" Crockett, 1786-1836, of Tennessee, a frontiersman, scout, soldier, and politician. Some folktales are about such mythical characters as Robin Hood in England, William Tell in Switzerland, Don Quixote of Spain, and Paul Bunyan, a hero "invented" by loggers of Minnesota and Wisconsin. Frequently men and women are inclined to enjoy a folktale but declare that there is no truth to the story. And, they are equally inclined to tell the story after becoming familiar with its details.

A selection of Italian, French, German, and Hispanic folktales is reproduced by Arthur M. Selvi, Lothar Kahn, and Robert C. Soule in their book, *Folklore Of Other Lands,* published in 1956.

Many of the folktales that have been repeated in the Western Hemisphere were brought by the Spanish. Those tales have long circulated in Florida, Louisiana, Texas, New Mexico, and California. The French, too, brought their folktales. The English brought such folktales as "Jack the Giant-Killer," and "Jack and the Bean Stalk." The Germans, Scotch-Irish, and the Irish who came to Pennsylvania, too, brought with them their own folktales.

Among the folktales best known in the United States are those about the lost continent of Atlantis, about Tom Quick the Indian slayer of Milford, Pennsylvania, Johnny Appleseed (John Chapman) of Massachusetts, Mike Fink (born in 1770 in the wilderness near present Pittsburgh, Pennsylvania) the last keelboatman, Captain Samuel Brady and his leap across a rock gorge in order to escape Indians, and the story of Rip Van Winkle, as later made famous by Washington Irving.

Eastern United States has had a large number of folktales about witches and ghosts. The South has had numerous Negro folktales, and the West a rich store of folktales of strange characters who had amazing physical strength and unbelievable skill in handling a rifle. Ghost stories have been popular not only in the East but also beyond the Mississippi. A collection of them comprises a volume, *Great Ghost Stories of the Old West,* 1968, edited by Betty Baker and published by Four Winds Press, New York.

Some folktales which seem in the 1970's to be totally inconceivable have passed from one European country to another for 2,000 years and on to America, and have been told in many versions.

Not until this century did the collecting of folktales in the United States make much progress. American folklorists from 1875 to 1920 spent much of their time on folksongs rather than on folktales. The American Folklore Society was founded in 1888 and the Pennsylvania Folklore Society, rather informally, in about the middle 1930's but was not incorporated until 1956. However, from the 1930's folktales have been collected systematically in the United States. In the 1930's Elizabeth Gardner was gathering folktales in the Scoharie Hills in upstate New York. Richard Chase brought out *Jack Tales,* 1943, and *Grandfather Tales,* 1948, about the Southern Appalachians. Vance Randolph's writings about the folktales of the Ozarks have been appearing from 1947.

From at least 1912 and probably a few years earlier, (preceding Gardner, Chase, and Randolph), and on through the 1930's, Henry Wharton Shoemaker was collecting folktales as told in the mountains of Central Pennsylvania. He published a large number of tales in book and in pamphlet form. An extensive list of those publications, and general comments about his collecting and writing, can be found on pages 277-281 of my book, *Adventures and Philosophy of a Pennsylvania Dutchman.*

Some folktales are based in part on history, some on history and the supernatural, and some seem to be entirely imaginative. Here are two examples of folktales based in part on history, and an example of each of the other two types, all four from Central Pennsylvania.

The *first example* is a Franklin County tale about a miraculous escape from Indians. Settlers living at the east foot of the Tuscarora Mountain in the late 1750's and early 1760's in what is now Peters Township were attacked by Indians at least eight times. The Indians, infuriated by the westward advance of white settlers, joined the French against the British in a struggle known as the French and Indian War. The Indians burned Matthew Patton's house and barn, the location of which was later the site of Fort Loudoun. After that incident and before the Fort Loudoun stockade was built in 1756 a man named Alexander was pursued by Indians. The tale insists that Alexander escaped by jumping across the West Branch of the Conococheague Creek. The details are not clear.

Thomas F. Gordon tells us that on the evening of February 29, 1756, "a party of Indians were discovered by one Alexander, near the house of Thomas Barr, in Peters township. Alexander was pursued, but escaped, and alarmed the fort at M'Dowel's mill, and notice of the presence of the enemy was speedily given to the township." (*The History of Pennsylvania, From Its Discovery by Europeans to the Declaration of Independence in 1776*, Philadelphia, 1829, page 616).

The same information is given by I. D. Rupp, in almost identical words. (*The History and Topography of Dauphin, Cumberland, Franklin, Bedford, Adams, Perry, Somerset, Cambria & Indiana Counties*, Lancaster, 1848, page 101). In 1887, Warner, Beers & Company, Chicago, brought out its large volume, *History of Franklin County, Pennsylvania.* That volume stated on page 169 that on February 29, 1756, "a man named Alexander discovered a party of Indians near Thomas Barr's place, in Peters Township," but did not mention that Alexander was pursued by Indians and that he escaped. The 1887 volume, however, had a list of taxables of Peters Township, for 1786. The list includes the following persons having Alexander as their first or last name: Daniel Alexander, Andrew Alexander, Hez. Alexander, Arthur Alexander, Alexander Brown, Alexander Hutchison, Alexander McKee, Alexander Robertson, David Alexander, and Alexander McConnel. (Pages 568-569). It is reasonable to believe that thirty years before, there was at least one person by the name of Alexander living within the township.

The legend has it that Alexander made the jump from a rather high bank of the creek, a short distance below the site where the stockade for Fort Loudoun was later erected. The "channel" is the probable location of the jump. At that point the creek bank is high on one side and low on the other. Mrs. Eugene Etter of Lemasters, Pennsylvania, grew up on a farm in the locality and she remembers small islands in the creek at the "channel," nearly sixty years ago. By jumping to that nearest island instead of wading, especially if the water was high at the time, Alexander could have gained the few minutes that saved his life.

This folktale passed from generation to generation in the Dickey family, in Peters Township, Franklin County. Perhaps Alexander was a member of that family. Various members of that prominent Dickey family are buried in Spring Grove Cemetery, three-fourth of a mile west of Lemasters, less than thirty feet from the graves of the parents, and of two sisters, two brothers, and five other close relatives of James Buchanan, Fifteenth President of the United States.

Mr. Seth Dickey, who was born April 7, 1841, and died on April 15, 1925, was the last member of the Peters Township Dickey family. He told Mr. John L. Finafrock the story of Alexander's escape. Seth Dickey is buried in Fairview Cemetery, Mercersburg, Pennsylvania. Mr. Finafrock, Superintendent of Franklin County Schools, 1922-1934, and President of Kittochtinny Historical Society, 1925-1941, told the story to Mr. Eugene Etter, a Member of the Franklin County Planning Commission, who, in turn, told it to me.

Here is the *second example* of a Central Pennsylvania folktale that is based in part on history. The tale credits Robert McClellan as being the "World's Greatest Athlete." McClellan was the son of a farmer in Peters Township, Franklin County. The boy was born on a farm approximately two miles west of Mercersburg on what is now known as Johnston's Lane.

According to local lore, when McClellan was a youth there was a hard slate section of road at what is now, 1974, the location of the Mountain View Elementary School, about six miles from McClellan's home. That hard slate section of road was known as the race track and races of various kinds were held there during McClellan's youth. On that race track he took a running jump, leaping over a Conestoga wagon, a freight wagon with a high tent-like cover. Later McClellan was in Colonel Daniel Brodhead's 8th Pennsylvania Regiment at time of the successful expedition against the Muskingum Indians in what is now the State of Ohio. While in the Ohio country with Brodhead a field day was held and on that occasion, again, according to the tale, McClellan jumped over a Conestoga wagon.

Charles McKnight wrote and compiled a large volume, *Our Western Border*, published in Philadelphia and in Chambersburg, Pennsylvania, in 1875. In that volume McKnight stated that McClellan "was one of the most athletic and active men on foot that has appeared on this globe." (Page 555). McKnight continued, "On the grand parade at Fort Greenville ‡Ohio†, where the ground was very little inclined, to show his activity, he ‡Robert McClellan† leaped over a road wagon with the cover stretched over; the wagon and bows were eight and a half feet high." (Page 555). McKnight also stated:

> Many marvelous stories are related of his ‡Robert McClellan's† athletic exploits. While at Fort Hamilton, he would frequently leap over the tallest horse without apparent exertion. In the town of Lexington, Ky., when passing along a narrow sidewalk with Matthew Heuston, a yoke of oxen happened to be drawn up on the sidewalk and instead of walking around them, as did his companion, he, without a moment's hesitation, leaped over both at a bound. (Pages 565-566).

On pages 554-570 McKnight has much to say about the fabulous Robert McClellan, including McClellan's trapping on the Missouri River and travelling west with the Astoria Expedition. Washington Irving's *Astoria* (two volumes, Philadelphia, 1836, compiled with the assistance of Irving's nephew, Pierre) mentions McClellan in chapters 13, 14, 19, 35, 38, 46, and 47. Washington Irving stated:

> M'Lellan [sic] was a remarkable man. He had been a partisan under General Wayne, in his Indian wars, where he had distinguished himself by his fiery spirit and reckless daring, and marvelous stories were told of his exploits. His appearance answered to his character. His frame was meagre, but muscular; showing strength, activity, and iron firmness. His eyes were dark, deep set, and piercing. He was restless, fearless, but of impetuous and sometimes ungovernable temper. (This description from the edition of *Astoria* published in 1900 by R. F. Fenno & Co., New York City, pages 109-110).

Even though Washington Irving does not tell of Robert McClellan's athletic prowess he does tell of McClellan's endurance during periods of extended physical strain on the trek from the Missouri River to the Pacific Ocean. Perhaps Charles McKnight's written accounts and the oral tradition about McClellan's athletic prowess might be largely true but somewhat overdrawn. Folktales need not be exact, but history must be precise to be worth anything.

The *third example* is a folktale based on history and the supernatural. In northwestern Bedford County in 1856 the death of two brothers, George and Joseph Cox, aged 7 and 5 years respectively, founded a legend known as "The Lost Children of the Alleghenies." The two boys lost their way in the forest near their father's farm and died of exposure and starvation. The boys became lost on April 24. Searching parties scoured the mountains in an effort to find them. It was estimated that more than two thousand people were looking for the lost children. It is said that magicians were asked to use their "special powers" to help find the boys. But all to no avail. On the tenth night after the disappearance of the Cox children a man who lived approximately twelve miles from the Cox home, Jacob Dibert, dreamed he was looking for the lost children and that he found them—dead. After Dibert dreamed the same dream two more times he told the dream to his brother-in-law, Harrison Whysong, who knew from Dibert's description the area to which the dream led. The two men followed the trail exactly as unfolded in the dream, and on May 8 found the two boys, dead.

In nearly a century and a quarter the "legend" of "The Lost Children of the Alleghenies" grew. In 1906 a monument was erected at the site where the children were found. Their gravestone can be seen in the hillside cemetery beside the small church in Pavia in Bedford County where they were buried. A countless number of people have visited both the site where the boys were found and their final resting place.

In about 1935 I visited a brother of "The Lost Children of the Alleghenies." He was then an elderly man living on Bedford Street in Johnstown, Pennsylvania. In 1938 the first edition of the *Guidebook To Historic Places in Western Pennsylvania* [western *half* of the state] published by the University of Pittsburgh Press, discussed the Cox children. (Page 41).

The story of "The Lost Children of the Alleghenies" has been told orally in hundreds of families in Bedford and neighboring Counties. It has also been told in numerous newspaper articles, as for example in the Harrisburg *Telegraph*, Saturday Supplement, July 11, 1938, and the Philadelphia *Record* for August 8, 1938.

At the annual Memorial Services for the Cox children held at Pavia on July 2, 1939, Rev. Elmer A. Dech presented a poem of six stanzas, "Pathos Of 1856," which he wrote the night before. The last stanza, as published in the Bedford *Gazette* for July 14, 1939, is as follows.

The dreamer, Mr. Jacob Dibert by name,
Had risen from obscurity to fame.
So now, the Allegheny mystery was solved,
And peace and comfort came to all involved.
But the moral of the sad tale does still remain,
And may be repeated again and again.
Children, do not venture from paths away,
For dreamers are few who find those astray.

Among the many articles concerning the Cox children was one in the Johnstown *Tribune-Democrat* for August 5, 1958. Entitled "Legend Grows, 'Lost Children' Not Forgotten," by Robert G. Rice, it included three photographs. (Page 2). And the legend continues, with many people declaring positively that Jacob Dibert's dream accomplished what more than two thousand searchers could not accomplish.

The *fourth example* is a folktale of the entirely imaginative type. In Franklin and other Central Pennsylvania Counties the story of the Ewiga Yeager (Eternal Hunter) was told among the Pennsylvania Germans. It is an ancient tale that was perpetuated by German folklore and was brought to Eastern Pennsylvania by the Germans who entered the Port of Philadelphia between 1683 and 1808. As they moved inland they carried this folktale with them.

The Ewiga Yeager (pronounced yeager, but spelled jaeger in standard German) said he would hunt until procuring much game. It was declared that the Lord held the hunter to his promise, and saw to it that the hunter was always unsuccessful. Therefore the Ewiga Yeager crossed the heavens night after night in search of game. In Central Pennsylvania and in numerous other places inhabited by the Pennsylvania Germans, men asserted for years that they could hear the Ewiga Yeager flying overhead but that they could not see him.

Interestingly, the Ewiga Yeager folktale is somewhat like the story of Orion in the mythology of the ancient Greeks. Orion, the son of Neptune, was a giant and a mighty hunter. He rose to fame, and then fortune turned eternally against him. Today he is remembered because of a star in the sky that is named for him. That star chases across the heavens in the beginning of winter, throughout the night. In the beginning of summer it can be seen at daybreak in the east.

° ° ° ° ° °

The folktales included in the remainder of this book seem to be a combination of European folktales and mountain life in Central Pennsylvania in the last half of the nineteenth century. In a sense these stories form a bridge between our sophisticated way of life in the 1970's and the primitive origins from which we sprang in Medieval Europe. In the 1970's the folktales of a hundred or more years ago seem so unbelievable that one wonders why they were repeated from generation to generation down to the time of our grandparents. In the nineteenth century and into the early years of the twentieth, Americans, even in urban areas, were much more superstitious than they are today. The emphasis on science and its accompanying explosion of knowledge, especially during and after World War II, largely undercut the superstitious beliefs on which many of the folktales were based.

To the best of my knowledge the following folktales have never been published except in my series of articles in 1934 and 1935, now reprinted here, and the five of them that were reprinted in *Keystone Folklore Quarterly*. Neither in 1934-1935 nor since then have I embellished those stories in any way. They are genuine. As mentioned in the Preface, included with those stories are two collected by Dr. George Swetnam. Those two, entitled "The Purring Panthers," and "Cherry Tree Joe McCreery," are delightful narratives. Like the stories of 1934 and 1935, the two Swetnam stories were published previously and are reprinted here exactly as published originally.

The map shows the locale of ten of the folktales.

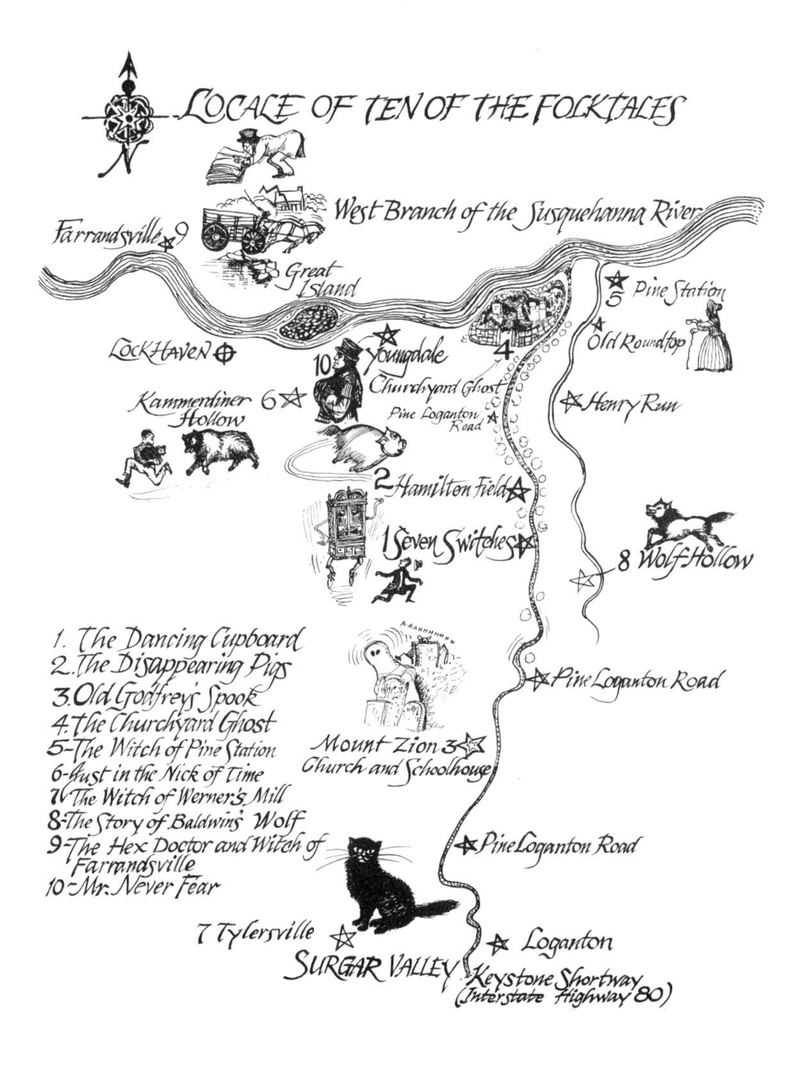

VI

The Dancing Cupboard

The Pine-Loganton road extends from Pine Station to Loganton, in southeastern Clinton County. The road winds from the Susquehanna River, up over rugged and picturesque mountains, and descends to Sugar Valley. The road crosses the "divide" which separates the West Branch Valley on the north, Sugar Valley on the south, Nippenose Valley on the east, and Nittany Valley on the west. The road is twelve miles in length and is a dirt road except for the last two miles, which dip down into Loganton. One may travel for long distances on this road without seeing anything except mountains, sky and woods. In fact one is more likely to see a deer, a gray squirrel or a ruffed grouse than a person, on parts of this road, on the other hand parts of this road traverse a farming section.°

Many interesting events have occurred along the Pine-Loganton road, and among the people up on the divide. A number of these stories have been told to me by residents who claim they were actual witnesses. I have jotted a few of these stories down. The scene of a number of the following stories is laid in this beautiful mountainous Pine-Loganton section. I am writing the stories as they were told to me and am mentioning the exact places at which each event was supposed to have taken place. In some instances I have changed the names of the characters so as to avoid offense to these people or to their living relatives. The following story, concerning the "Dancing Cupboard" is one of the strangest "spook stories" that I have yet heard.

About fifty-five years ago [in the neighborhood of 1879], a young girl of about eighteen years was employed as housekeeper for a man in McElhattan. This man was approximately thirty-five years of age. He forced the girl to forge her father's name to a note. The girl's father, detecting the fraud and intimidation, threatened to punish the McElhattan man. The

° The road had a heavy traffic in the heyday of lumbering on the top of the Bald Eagle Mountain in the last two decades of the nineteenth century. Many teams hauled saw logs down to Pine Station where they were formed into rafts and floated on the West Branch of the Susquehanna River. Some of those rafts went to sawmills at Williamsport and others went on down the West Branch to the main stem of the Susquehanna at Sunbury, and down the Susquehanna to Marietta in Lancaster County, where they were purchased by lumber merchants.

girl's home was in Sugar Valley. One day the man started out with his housekeeper, on the way to the girl's home. He returned to McElhattan in a few days but the girl was never seen again. She was last seen at "The Seven Switches," a junction of roads at a lonely spot on the Pine-Loganton road, with the employer, on that fateful trip, leading away from McElhattan.°

THE FOREST AREA IN WHICH THE SEVEN SWITCHES WERE LOCATED

From a photograph taken in 1974. The location has been made unsightly by a recent lumbering operation. The foreground of the picture is the location of the Seven Switches. They were near the highest point on the Pine-Loganton road.

° At "The Seven Switches" the Pine-Loganton Road became particularly soft in the spring of the year under the traffic of many wagonloads of logs. As the road became deeply rutted, the wagoners drove to one side of the soft spot. As the new passing point, or switch, became soft, the wagoners drove to one side of the two soft spots, and so on until there were seven "switches."

The man returned to his home in McElhattan but said nothing about the girl. In a week's time the man disappeared, taking his possessions with him, and was never heard of again. It was rumored that he had murdered the girl.

About twenty-five years later a descendent of one of the old-time mountaineers had a very distressing experience in the neighborhood of the Seven Switches. This person, a George Hanson, was 16 or 18 years old at the time. He had been "keeping company" with a certain young girl, a Mary Bitner by name. The Hanson farm and the Bitner farm are nestled high up in the mountains, separated by more than two miles of woods. George was coming home from the Bitner farm one night about midnight.

The moon was shining brightly. When he came to the Seven Switches, a point on the Pine road just about three quarters of a mile from his home, he saw a large object appear suddenly, directly in front of him, in the middle of the road. He looked at it intently and noticed that it was a fine old four-sided cupboard with glass doors. It was filled with dishes, beautiful dishes of finest china and of all colors, he claims to this day. The dishes were standing on end, supported by racks, and they were arranged in even rows. The moonlight shone beautifully on the rare collection of china pieces.

There were white curtains inside of the glass doors of the cupboard. The curtains were tied back with narrow silk ribbons of a red color, and the curtained windows made a dainty setting for the elegant dishes. George was wide-eyed and dumb-founded with amazement and admiration. But where did this cupboard and these costly dishes come from? Why did they appear so suddenly and in such a lonely spot, and at such an unearthly hour?

These questions puzzled George sorely, but in another moment the cupboard started grotesque antics. The cupboard began to dance, right before the startled man. And how it did dance! It pranced from side to side, then backward. The cupboard was beautiful and the china was of priceless quality. The rays of the moonlight glimmered on the polished cupboard and sparkled on the rich glazed surface of the china. It was a spectacle to behold. But George had passed the stage of amazement and admiration. He was becoming frightened, but he was unable to run.

Gradually the dancing cupboard danced toward him. Closer and closer it came. It seemed to be growing arms. Were these arms reaching out to seize him? George became horrified. The cupboard made a quick step toward George and extended those gruesome arms further than before. George gave a leap. He ran towards home. The cupboard danced ahead of him. He jumped to the side of the road and tried to pass the cupboard, but it kept ahead of him, between him and home, sweet home. Should he turn

GEORGE HANSON SEES THE DANCING CUPBOARD

and run in the other direction? No. Home was the nearest haven of refuge. So in spite of the fact that the Dancing Cupboard danced in front of him George continued his flight towards the Hanson farm.°

This Dancing Cupboard! It moved so gracefully. It did not careen as it danced and danced along. At times it seemed to withdraw those ugly arms, and, even smile, just a bit. And those dishes! How beautiful they were, with the moonlight playing on them. But George could not appreciate those things at the moment. The cupboard danced along ahead of him for about sixty or seventy yards. And then, the cupboard went SMASH. It fell down on the ground before the terrified youth, with a sickening and thundering crash, making as much noise as though it had been hurled to a cobblestone street from a fourth-story window.

George tried to run faster than before but, as luck would have it, he stumbled and fell flat on the ground the moment the cupboard crashed. The doors of the cupboard flew open and the dishes fell out, rolling all around the stricken boy. He tried to get on his feet and run again but he crawled rapidly for about sixty yards before he was able to regain an erect position. Then he quickened his speed. He ran and ran. He took a short cut through what is known as the Hamilton field, and ran on through brush and briers until he arrived at his father's door. He did not stop to open the door. He fell against it, terrified and exhausted. The door gave away to the impact of his body and he fell headlong into the room, frightening those of the family who had not yet retired for the night.

George was a sorry looking mess. His bare knees poked out through large holes in his "best pants," his clothes were torn, and his face and hands were badly scratched, because of his hasty short cut through brush and briers. When he was sufficiently composed his father was able to draw the story of the Dancing Cupboard out of him, bit by bit. The old man gave a weighty decision—the cupboard was the ghost of the murdered serving girl, the housekeeper from Sugar Valley.

° The "Hanson" farm, a third of a mile from the Pine-Loganton Road, is located on a broad, high shelf, at the south foot of the north face of the Bald Eagle Mountain in Wayne Township, Clinton County. Locally, this high ridge of the Bald Eagle Mountain in Wayne Township is known as McElhattan Knob, Simcox Mountain, and Mount Darlington. The view in several directions from the house at the "Hanson" farm is gorgeous but is somewhat difficult to capture with a camera. The house is surrounded by about forty acres of land that may have been farmed successfully in the 1890's or shortly thereafter. Since at least 1932 those acres that could produce farm products have been almost wholly neglected. The present house replaces a more attractive old one that was destroyed by fire about 1965.

In successive years other people have claimed that they saw the Dancing Cupboard at night near the Seven Switches. Some report that they saw it only at a distance and heard the china dishes rattle in a weird and horrible way.

Such are the stories of the Dancing Cupboard.

VII

The Disappearing Pigs

THE "STRANGE" ANIMALS

"The Hamilton Field" is an abandoned clearing along the "Pine road," in Wayne Township, between Pine Station and Loganton, in the southern part of Clinton County.° According to some of my friends several mysterious events have taken place in this vicinity. About fifty years ago a family by the name of Hamilton lived on this small tract of mountain land

° There are two fields, the upper being approximately five acres in area and the lower about two acres. In 1974 those fields are separated by a strip of woods approximately eighty feet wide. Much of the upper field and nearly all of the lower have been reseeded by the forest. In 1932 the two fields were fairly open. There were apple trees, and a cellar and foundation walls of a farmhouse.

In the spring of 1973 Mr. Lewis Wilson of Pine Station, who was born in August 1881, remembered the Hamilton Place being farmed in about 1891. At that time he saw apples being picked in its orchard. Apple trees then grew slowly, indicating that the farm may have been established as much as twenty years earlier. Mr. Wilson saw a farmhouse, a barn and a sundial at the Hamilton Place.

and farmed it. For the past thirty-five or forty years the farm has been deserted. Today the only remaining evidence which would indicate that the clearing was at one time a farm and a homestead is a forsaken and dying apple orchard. All traces of buildings disappeared years ago.

Almost forty years ago [about 1894], one moonlight night, at eight or nine o'clock, a mountain boy of about fifteen years was walking through the woods a half mile from the Hamilton Field. He suddenly became aware of the fact that a wildcat was crouching on the limb of a tree over his head, ready to spring down on him. He became frightened and ran as rapidly as his legs would carry him. He had a gun in his pocket, but because of his bewilderment he forgot all about the gun. He ran until he came to the Hamilton Field. By that time he had "run the scare" out of himself. He slowed down to a walk and continued on his way home. As he was crossing the Hamilton Field he saw two white animals. He thought they were small pigs. He tried to catch them and came within ten feet of them. Each of the two animals was covered with long white hair. They had short pugged snouts and their eyes seemed to be in the top of their heads rather than in the front, for as the boy stared down on the animals they looked directly up at him without as much as raising their heads. He said they resembled poodle dogs. Before he had an opportunity to grasp either one of these odd animals both of them disappeared.

The next morning he told the story to two of his brothers. That afternoon they took their two dogs, a bull dog and a blood hound, and watched the Hamilton Field, hoping the mysterious animals would reappear. At two o'clock that afternoon the animals were again sighted, but the three boys could not get very close to the little white creatures. The boys and the dogs watched the field the next two afternoons. Each afternoon at two o'clock they spied the strange white pair, but they could not get within close range of the animals. On the fourth afternoon they decided to pen the dogs in the deserted Hamilton barn, thinking that the mysterious animals gave them a wide berth because of the presence of the dogs. It was agreed among the boys that one of them should stay at the barn with

---

Mrs. Mary Sour Gardner of Pine Station walked with others to the Hamilton Fields in about 1916 and found that the Hamilton Place had already been abandoned. Mrs. Gardner has a deed (indenture) from John B. Newman and wife to one Alexander Hamilton dated September 5, 1845, for land in Wayne Township, 311 acres, "more or less," together with "all and singular the Houses & Buildings," for $100.00, being the piece of land called "Liberty." The "Liberty" tract had been granted to Thomas Brown in 1792 by the Commonwealth. From Brown it passed to Alexander Hamilton, and then to John Hamilton, his son. A transcript of taxes dated May 9, 1870, shows that a John Hamilton had paid taxes on unseated land in Clinton County. G. W. Sour, Mrs. Gardner's grandfather, was the next owner of the Hamilton Place. Mrs. Gardner's father and mother sold the Hamilton Fields to Colonel Henry W. Shoemaker in or about 1916.

the dogs while the other two would station themselves in the field at some distance from the barn. If the mysterious "pigs" would approach the two boys in the field, then one of the boys in the field would whistle to the boy in the barn, thus signalling to him to turn the dogs loose.

PINE-LOGANTON ROAD AT THE HAMILTON FIELDS, 1974

The road was a busy thoroughfare in the 1880's and 1890's. In the 1930's the northern half of the Pine-Loganton road was nearly abandoned, and was covered with a blanket of grass. In the late 1950's and early 1960's the Wayne Township Supervisors widened and began to pike the road with stones. In 1974 much of the road is hard-packed, as shown here, and has a blacktop surface from Mount Zion to the highway that enters Loganton.

The strange animals appeared at exactly two o'clock. They evidently sensed no danger. They drew closer and closer to the two excited boys in the field. Then—a whistle, the opening of the barn door, and the barking and dashing of the dogs. The white animals became frightened and ran

THE DISAPPEARING PIGS

down a slope, the dogs following them at full speed. The three boys followed as rapidly as they could make their way through the field and the adjoining woods. In a few minutes the chase had come to an end. The boys caught up to the dogs. The dogs were standing under a jack pine tree in a cleared spot in a hollow. The dogs were barking and standing on their hind legs, scratching on the tree trunk, just as coon dogs do when they have "treed" their quarry. They want to climb the tree and get their coon. They know they cannot climb yet they try to reach as far up the tree as they can. In this case the bull dog and the blood hound struggled furiously to get up into the tree. Evidently they had treed the two white pigs. The tree was only about five inches in diameter and no other tree was within sixty or seventy feet of it. The pigs were not in the tree. They were nowhere in sight when the three boys arrived. But the pine tree was swinging back and forth when they arrived on the scene, just as though some one or some thing had jumped out of the branches only a moment before.

The story is told that these white pigs were seen twice before the scared boy saw them. Two years before the animals were "treed" they were seen by a man who was driving down the Pine road, with a horse and wagon. The pigs crossed the road a short distance in front of his horse, near the Hamilton Field. Two months before the pigs were "treed" another person had seen the peculiar animals in the Hamilton Field. But it seems that no one has ever seen the "Disappearing Pigs" since they were "treed." What has become of them? Perhaps the working of a disappearance in mid air was too much for them and taxed their supernatural powers to the breaking point.

In answer to my queries as to an explanation of the antics of these "Disappearing Pigs" the person who was scared by the wild cat and amazed by the pigs years ago simply shook his head and, with a faraway look, said, "I'll be blamed if I ever could figger it out myself."

VIII

Old Godfrey's Spook

Mt. Zion is a beautiful little farming community in the southern part of our county. This community is located in the vicinity of the Pine-Loganton road, midway between Pine Station and Loganton. It is perched up on the mountains which separate the West Branch, Nittany, Nippenose, and Sugar Valleys.

Mt. Zion Church and Mt. Zion school house, with their neatly kept yards, snug and comfortable appearance, stand side by side, along the "Pine Road," and form the center of the community, surrounded by a number of farms scattered about within a two or three-mile radius. Mt. Zion was a bustling place in the lumbering days. Many of the older residents of this section, of a generation or more ago, were superstitious and believed in ghosts.

In days gone by a number of ghost stories originated in this section. The grave yard at Mt. Zion had seen its ghost. A farm house in the community had been reported as being "haunted." It was said that a certain family in the community had suffered under the curse of a witch. And a little gully along the Pine Road, about a half mile north of the church still bears the name of Spook Hollow. Mt. Zion was fairly well steeped in superstition.

A Mr. "Jim" Sheasley is a native of Mt. Zion and has lived in that community almost continuously since he was sixteen years old. He is a hearty and active man in his early sixties. He has farmed and worked in the lumber camps in the vicinity of Mt. Zion. As a boy and as a young man he had heard the stories of ghosts that were told at Mt. Zion. One dark night, about a dozen years ago, he received a bad scare. The Mt. Zion ghost stories that he had heard time and again played on his mind and for a few minutes, made a bad situation considerably worse. Here is the story as he told it to me.

Robert Godfrey died in 1922, at the age of 85. For the last four years of his life he was an invalid and was confined to his bed. During the last year and a half of his life he was delirious, calling constantly in his waking hours, "Mom, Mom, Mom." He lived in Robins Hollow with his family. His closest neighbors lived about one quarter of a mile away and often these "next door neighbors" could hear the old man sending up his un-

OLD GODFREYS' SPOOK

ceasing wail. The old man's condition was serious and no one was permitted to visit him. Gradually the people in the community began to believe that Old Godfrey had committed a serious crime in days gone by and that the family barred visitors, fearing that the old man might reveal his crime while delirious, or in a sane moment when death would stare him in the face.

When Robert Godfrey died he was buried in the grave yard at Mt. Zion Church. Several days after the burial of the old man, "Jim" Sheasley was walking home along the "Pine Road." At that time Sheasley lived on a farm about a fourth of a mile from the Godfrey farm. He had been working at a saw mill on Spring Run and his walk took him past the grave yard. It was about seven or eight o'clock and the night was pitch dark. As Jim passed the old school house and came in sight of the church and the grave yard he saw a sight that held him breathless. In the grave yard he beheld a white figure flapping its arms slowly.

Jim was bolted fast to the ground. He stood and watched the weird figure. He couldn't run. He couldn't call for help. What was this figure? Was it Old Godfrey's spook? What else could it be? Hadn't he heard a great deal about the ghosts of Mt. Zion? Jim was held by the spell of the phantom image. The white thin arms drooped. They hung still and limp. Then, suddenly, they raised again and fluttered in an unconcerned way. The "spook" did not chase Jim. It did not throw any stones at him. It did not even screech at him.

Jim was no believer in "spooks." Yet the mysterious Old Godfrey had been buried in that small grave yard less than one week before.

Jim reasoned, as quickly as a petrified man can reason, that after all if the uncanny figure was actually a "spook" it could not hurt him. He wanted to see whether this fantastic object was a ghost. He watched a bit longer. Then he called to the eerie looking creature. But no answer came. Was it hard of hearing? Jim mustered more courage and called louder. But still no answer. Jim's courage rose a few more notches. He advanced a few steps toward the spook. The spook raised its arms once more and then left them sag again. Another step, two more steps, yet the spook remained at the same spot in the grave yard.

Jim was now both anxious and courageous. He walked stealthily but deliberately to the grave yard. And the mystery of Old Godfrey's spook was soon explained. A newspaper had been caught under the gate of the grave yard. The white newspaper stood out against the blackness of the night and the free ends of the paper rose and fell in the gentle breeze. Jim Sheasley was much relieved and Robert Godfrey has probably been resting peacefully ever since.

IX

The Church Yard Ghost

Pine Station can boast of a long list of old time woodsmen, hunters and good story tellers. Most of them have passed away by this time, but a few of the old guard still hang on. I have had many long and interesting talks with one of these old timers, Mr. Frank Edgar. Edgar is now in his seventy-sixth year. He is a venerable looking old man, with long white hair and whiskers. In his younger days he travelled with a circus, lumbered, and in later years did a great deal of landscape gardening. His stories of the Civil War, of circus days, of lumbering operations and miscellaneous events occurring in and about Pine have often held my attention. At present this old native of Pine is bedfast in the Lock Haven Hospital. I have visited him at the Hospital a number of times in the past few weeks, and, instead of my entertaining him, he has entertained me, by reminiscing about old times. One story in particular which he told me a few weeks ago held my attention. It concerned the Ghost of the old Evangelical Church near Pine Station.

The story has interested me. It is different from most ghost stories. It seems that usually a ghost selects a favorite church yard and hovers about it. But here is a story of a congregation which built its two successive church buildings on ground that was generally known to be "haunted."

Today one can see a small cemetery along the river bank about three-quarters of a mile west of Pine. But no church is in sight.

There are no buildings of any kind near the grave yard, which is known as the Stamm cemetery. There are a few ornamental evergreens inside the fence. To the west of the enclosure can be seen the foundations of the old church. Years ago a large white oak stood on the river bank east of and near to the present grave yard. For years the river currents had been undermining the bank in the neighborhood of the Stamm cemetery, so that the bank and the old oak tree which grew upon it were washed away, probably thirty years ago. At the time the bank and the oak were washed away, the tree was about twenty inches in diameter and forty feet high.

According to my good friend, a man hanged himself on the white oak tree about seventy years ago. A few years after the suicide was committed, the Evangelicals built their church on the foundation which visitors can see today, near what was then the site of the white oak tree. The congregation opened a grave yard and buried their dead outside their church.

Years ago a dispute occurred between the two bishops of the Evangelical Church—Bishop Dubbs and Bishop Esher. The litigation attracted much attention in the denomination and divided many Evangelical congregations into two factions, the Dubbsites and the Esherites. The Evangelical congregation at Pine Station accordingly lined up, some on the side of Dubbs and others on the side of Esher. The Esherites formed the majority and they gained control of the Pine Evangelical Church. These Pine Esherites disregarded the Pine Dubbsites, tore down the church building and took the furniture and lumber to Sugar Valley, where they erected a church building of their own. The Dubbsites built another church on the old foundation next to the white oak tree near Pine. In 1910 this Evangelical Church was struck by lightning and destroyed by fire. It has never been rebuilt.°

Many of the old residents of Pine, thirty and forty years ago, believed that the Evangelical grave yard was haunted by the ghost of the man who hanged himself on the white oak tree. A number of these residents claimed that they had seen the ghost in the vicinity of the grave yard on dark nights. Some saw the ghost in the form of a man, some in the form of a dog, and some in the form of a deer. One man claimed for years that the ghost appeared to him in the form of a deer and also claimed that it was the cursed white oak that saved his life. The ghost in the form of a deer lunged at him. He dodged behind the tree just in the nick of time. The deer lunged at him again. And a third time, and a fourth time, the tree saved his life. So the terrified man publicly claimed to the end of his life.

My friend in the Hospital left me to understand that spooks and ghosts were all a matter of one's imagination, and that he did not believe in such mystical goings-on. He had heard many tales of haunted places but called all these stories foolishness. He told me, however, that one night he himself received a bad scare when coming down the old river road from "Goat Hill School House" to Pine. The night was dark and he had to pass the haunted grave yard and the white oak tree. As he came near the grave yard he suddenly looked up. He saw a figure resembling a man, just a little distance ahead of him, coming toward him. He thought nothing of the matter and continued on his way. In a few moments he looked ahead again, and sure enough, the figure had disappeared COMPLETELY. Mr.

° There is probably an error of fact here. According to three people who have been residents of Pine Station for many years the first church building was struck by lightning and destroyed by fire and the second church building was torn down and moved away. However, I am giving the story as my aged friend gave it to me.

It seems that the factions in the congregation resulted in a dying-off of membership and enthusiasm, and that the church building was sold, torn down and shipped to a mission in Northumberland, Pa., near Sunbury, about the year 1910.

THE GHOST VANISHES AND MR. EDGAR THROWS STONES DOWN THE RIVER BANK

Edgar now thought to himself, "Someone who knows me is trying to play a trick on me. That person has slid down the steep river bank and is hiding from me. I'll fix him." So Mr. Edgar picked up a large stone, went to the edge of the river and called out, commanding the unknown person to show his face or brave a fusillade of stones. There was no answer. Mr. Edgar called again. But no answer. Mr. Edgar threw stones down the bank. But no answer, no cry of pain; no sound except the echo of the noisy stones, and the pounding of Mr. Edgar's heart! Who or what was this figure? Why had it vanished so quickly and completely? Were the old stories of the Church Yard Ghost true after all? These were the questions that ran through Mr. Edgar's mind.

And he told me confidentially, "There's nothing to this spook business, but that's the closest I ever came to seeing a ghost."

X

The Make-Believe Ghost

Thirty years ago Clinton County was teeming with lumber camps and "lumber jacks." This section of Pennsylvania had great stands of valuable white pine and hemlock timber. Most of this timber has disappeared and with it have gone the lumber camps with all their glamour, color, and glory. Lumbering was done in a big way. Miles of railroad were built through the forest to haul logs to the mill and hundreds of camps dotted the mountains. These camps were composed of sturdy men who for the most part were as cordial and jovial as they were strong and hard-working. They ate their meals in one large room, spent their evenings around the "block stove" in the "lobby" of the camp and slept in the bunk rooms. After supper on long winter evenings these men would tip back on their chairs in the lobby, watch the flickering lights filtering out from the holes in the glowing block stove, and listen to one of their number tell a story. Some of the stories told by the old lumbermen in the camps on cold winter evenings when a group of woodsmen were huddled around the lobby stove are highly entertaining.

The Clinton County lumberman of twenty or thirty years ago possessed the great quality of being able to tell stories that fascinate a listener and hold his undivided attention. During the past few years I have had the privilege to associate with quite a number of these real woodsmen, a type of people so often discovered in our mountains in Clinton County. Near Pine Station there lives a man whom I consider to be a typical woodsman of the good old type, a Mr. Flem Simcox. He lives on a small farm high above the Susquehanna River. His farm is part way up the side of the Bald Eagle Mountain and it overlooks the beautiful little village of Pine Station. This woodsman goes about his farming duties but he often sighs for "the good old days" in the woods and camps and enjoys talking about those old days.

Two winters ago I spent a particularly pleasant evening with this man in his kitchen. After eating a man-sized supper we pulled our chairs up close to the kitchen stove and leaned back comfortably. "Flem" was in a story telling humor. In vivid phrases he described life in the lumber camps and told some of his woods experiences, and stories that he had heard in the camps. Unfortunately many of these good stories have a way of fading in one's memory but the following story has stuck with me. Flem heard the story in camp years ago and he passed it on to me in these or similar words.

HOSKIN'S CAMP, EAST FORK OF SINNEMAHONING CREEK, POTTER COUNTY, PENNSYLVANIA

A typical Central Pennsylvania lumber camp of the late 1800's. From a photograph preserved by the former Pennsylvania Department of Forests and Waters and now preserved in the Archives Tower in Harrisburg.

"We were in camp one winter, and as busy as usual. Most of us were young then, wiry and full of mischief. We played lots of pranks on each other, laughed when some one else found his bed full of burrs, or shoes full of water in the morning, and also laughed when we found that such pranks had been played on us. We were a jolly lot. There was one old fellow among us. His name was Charlie O'Riley. He was about sixty-two years old but looked much older. He was a regular woods hick. He had logged for years, had a grizzled face and had but one eye. We boys played many a prank on the poor old fellow but he was a good scout and took everything well. He was a joking fellow, and likeable. We learned to respect him a great deal. In the evenings he used to be the center of our group in the lobby. We all told stories but his were best. One night he told us about a little love affair of his. He told us that when he was about eighteen years old he thought quite a bit of a certain girl. But, unfortunately for Charlie, his brother Dave, who was of about the same age as Charlie O'Riley, liked the same girl. Dave was getting the inside track. He was seeing the girl more evenings than Charlie was seeing her. Charlie could tolerate the 'competition' no longer. He decided to take drastic steps to put an end to this 'monkey-business.'

"It happened that Dave regularly took a short cut through a cemetery on his way to see the girl. Charlie decided to ambush his brother and scare him thoroughly so that he would not venture out of doors at night in the future, and thus end the distressing 'competition.'

"Charlie lay in wait for his opportunity. One fine moonlight evening Dave started out to make his call on the girl. He took the short cut through the cemetery as usual. Charlie followed him stealthily and at a safe distance, so that Dave would not see him. After Dave had passed beyond the cemetery Charlie selected a large tombstone and proceeded to make himself comfortable. He had business to attend to, and business which required a policy of 'watchful waiting.' He waited one hour, two hours, three hours, and yet no signs of Dave, or of anyone else. But Charlie was not discouraged. He was as patient as an Indian. He knew that Dave would pass through the cemetery on his way home.

"At last—a sound. What was it? Approaching footsteps. A pounding heart and straining eyes—yes, now Charlie could see the approaching figure, and it was Dave. Charlie now hastened to carry out his plans. He quickly pulled a neatly folded clean white sheet from under his coat. He threw it over himself, stood up between the tombstones in the moonlight and waved his sheet covered arms, uttered a few weird and ghost-like noises, a series of rising and falling staccato notes which sounded somewhat like the screeching of an owl, but a sound that was still more terrifying to an already stricken person, than an owl's screech would be.

"Charlie certainly must have looked and sounded like a real ghost, standing there in the grave yard in the moonlight, draped in a white sheet, and uttering such extraordinary sounds. Dave became frightened and did not stop to investigate. He ran from the cemetery as rapidly as he was able to run. But just as Charlie had attained this great success in his plans for the evening he heard a low and plaintive moaning directly behind him. The ghost himself became uneasy. He turned and—'what, w-w-wha-what is that?' He saw a white object only about twenty yards from him, between two grave stones. The white object stood out plainly in the moonlight and continued to moan. Charlie could not discern what the white object might be and he did not take time to investigate. He was thoroughly scared. He saw his brother disappearing at the edge of the cemetery, on the side towards HOME. The would-be ghost, Charlie, called out frantically, 'Wait a minute, Dave, I'll go with you!"

The next morning an innocent little sheep was found in the cemetery caught between two tombstones, and moaning pathetically.

"WAIT A MINUTE, DAVE, I'LL GO WITH YOU!"

XI

The Witch of Pine Station

In bygone days many people believed in sorcery, witchcraft and "the black art." In the late 1600's women in the New England states were sentenced to be hanged if they were suspected of possessing supernatural and magical powers of witchery. For many years natives of Pennsylvania have believed in the black art and hobgoblins. Today [1934] York County, Pennsylvania, is still a stronghold for superstitious beliefs. Less than ten years ago newspapers were filled with articles concerning the "hex doctors" and the superstitious beliefs found in York County.

Sixty years ago [in 1874] the belief in witches was much more widespread than it is today. Many of the people of Clinton County believed that some of their number were witches, who possessed dreadful and far-reaching powers. The following story concerns a woman of Pine Station who was considered by her neighbors to be a witch and a master of the black art. The story was told to me by a woman who knew the witch.

Pine Station was a flourishing little lumber town sixty years ago. The Stangs, the Bensons and the Hogans were three of the leading families in the community and these three families were closely related, all engaging in the lumber business. In addition to lumbering, the Hogans kept the Pine Station Hotel, a building which was destroyed by fire only a few years ago.°

A Susan Gahagan lived in Pine in those early days, inhabiting a small house all by herself. She was in general considered to be a respectable resident of the little town, but some people suspected that she was a witch and a sorceress. She was an incessant borrower. She would run often to a neighbor for a cup of sugar, or a "tin" of coffee or a scoop of flour. Many people in the community were of a superstitious nature and feared that Old Susan was a witch. These people did not refuse her when she came "a-borrowing" for they were afraid that she would cast a spell on them if they did.

° The Pine Station Hotel was a haven for raftsmen on the West Branch of the Susquehanna River. In the spring of the year when logs were being formed into rafts the Pine Station Hotel was a busy place, with as many as fifteen river pilots staying at the hotel at the same time. When rafting declined in the 1890's and during the first decade of the twentieth century the hotel lost some its business. Among its boarders were men who worked on the oil pipe line that passes through Pine Station, railroad station agents and signal tower operators, and railroad workers at the time the third track was being built through Pine Station. During the two-week Camp Meetings at Pine Camp Ground the hotel served as many as 300 meals per Sunday.

Old Susan often went to Grandmother Stang to borrow things. The Stangs were prosperous folks and Grandmother Stang was generous. She seldom refused Old Susan. The Bensons, however, were not so prosperous and lived a bit skimpily. They had to be thrifty to make ends meet. Consequently Grandmother Benson often refused to give flour and other articles to Old Susan when she came begging.

Grandmother Benson had a daughter by the name of Sarah. Sarah was about eighteen years old and the possessor of a beautiful saddle horse, of which she was very proud. One summer Old Susan had come "a-borrowing" to Sarah's mother quite frequently, and she was turned away empty-handed almost every time. Toward the latter part of the summer there were strange doings in the Benson barn. Each morning for about a week Sarah found her horse in the stable all sweated up, as though it had been ridden hard before dawn, and each time the horse's tail had been braided. All this in spite of her precaution each evening to see that the horse's tail was unbraided and that the animal was securely haltered and tied in its stall. But early on the succeeding mornings she found her horse with braided tail and a covering of lather.

The matter was talked around the family. Sarah's mother, Grandmother Benson, was a sister-in-law to Grandmother Stang, who had been born and raised in the hobgoblin atmosphere of York County and had come to Pine Station from there shortly before 1820. Grandmother Stang knew something about witchcraft, coming from the very citadel of the black art. And she pronounced at once with authority that Old Susan Gahagan was a witch and that she was visiting a curse on Grandmother Benson's daughter as a measure of vengeance for having been turned away when she begged for flour and other things.

Sarah Benson's horse was not molested after that summer and the incident was dropped. Sarah married a Mr. Samuel Hogan, and together they "kept hotel" in Pine. Sarah was exceptionally skilled in pie baking and her cooking won for the Pine Station Hotel quite an enviable reputation.

The hotel stood adjacent to the tracks of the Philadelphia and Erie Railroad (the Pennsylvania Railroad after May 1907, and in 1974 the Penn Central) and directly across from the railroad station. When a locomotive was "coaling up" at 11 o'clock one morning in 1923 it threw large sparks upward. The sparks ignited the hotel and it was destroyed almost at once, as was also the building adjacent to it, the store.

THE PINE STATION HOTEL

The structure (with five windows on second-story and two on third-story front) had thirteen rooms on the second floor. Five beds on the third floor were used when the hotel was crowded. The building with the second-story porch, next to the hotel, was the store and post office.

During the time that Sarah and Sam Hogan were running the hotel in Pine, in the early 1870's, Grandmother Stang raised two grandchildren at her home there. These two grandchildren were Henry and Kittie Stang, brother and sister, aged eight and six years respectively. Mr. and Mrs. Hogan were Uncle Sam and Aunt Sarah to the children, while their daughter, Betsy, aged nine years, was a cousin to the young Stang children. Henry and Kittie were very fond of their Aunt Sarah's pies and often trotted up the road to the hotel to see their aunt and cousin and also get a piece of pie.

One morning while the children were in the hotel kitchen with their aunt and cousin, they heard a terrific racket in the cellar. Hurrying to the cellar to see what happened, they found that the tierce of lard had been upset. In those days lard was kept in a wooden cask called a tierce, which held between sixty and seventy pounds. The tierce had been standing solidly on a firm table and could not have fallen to the floor as it did without being upset. The woman and the three children searched the cellar but could find no traces of anyone's being there. The outside door was securely locked and the inside door opened into the kitchen above.

Aunt Sarah and the children had been in the kitchen when the noise was heard. No person could have been in the cellar when the tierce was upset, and it could not have upset itself. How was this mysterious occurence to be explained? Grandmother Stang, the local authority on witchcraft, was consulted. After examining the cellar, the table, the cellar stairways and the tierce, she declared that the tierce had been bewitched by the sorceress, Old Susan Gahagan. She explained that first the witch had visited a curse on Sarah as a girl and now as a grown woman, as a measure of revenge upon Sarah's mother for refusing to give her what she begged. Grandmother Stang told Aunt Sarah Hogan to shoot a silver bullet into the tierce of lard, but she feared to do this, saying she was afraid it would result in the death of Old Susan. Then Grandmother Stang persuaded Aunt Sarah to thrust a red hot iron into the tierce, stating that through this act Old Susan's arm would be burned and the spell resting on the tierce would be removed. Grandmother Stang also told Mrs. Hogan that the witch would now lose her supernatural powers and would not be able to regain them until Mrs. Hogan would grant the witch a borrowing request.

The next day Old Susan came to the hotel and asked Aunt Sarah for a cup of sugar, saying she "was clean out of sugar today." Aunt Sarah noticed that the witch had her left arm bandaged. She told her firmly that she had no sugar to spare. Then the witch asked for a little coffee, but again Aunt Sarah was firm.

On the second and third days after the red hot iron application to the lard, the witch returned to the hotel, pleading to Aunt Sarah more

THE WITCH COMES "ABEGGING"

pathetically each time for "a little sugar," or "some coffee," or "a bit of flour." Mrs. Hogan pitied the witch and she finally gave in, loaning Old Susan a "tin of flour." That broke the curse that hung over the witch. Even so, no more sorcery was noticed in Pine for several months. About six months after that incident, little Betsy Hogan began to grow thin and puny. Doctors were consulted and she was given the best of food, but to no avail. After several months she was almost a skeleton and doctors were unable to diagnose the case. They were at a complete loss.

Again Grandmother Stang, with her York County knowledge of witchcraft, came to the rescue. She said Old Susan Gahagan had laid a curse upon the child—that she who had first placed her curse on the daughter was now placing it on the granddaughter—and that there was one way to remove the curse. Mrs. Hogan prepared a cup of tea every noontime for Betsy. And Old Susan drank her tea daily also. Grandmother Stang then said to Mrs. Hogan: "Take Betsy's cup of tea, put it in a bottle, cork it tightly and put it in the linen chest, plugging the key hole so as to make the chest air tight. As long as that tea is kept in the chest and the chest is kept air tight, the witch will be powerless." Mrs. Hogan followed Grandmother Stang's advice. Betsy's tea was bottled and corked tightly, then placed in Aunt Sarah's linen chest. The chest was locked and the keyhole tightly plugged.

The next afternoon Old Susan Gahagan came to the hotel and pleaded with Mrs. Hogan to pull the packing out of the key hole in the chest. She admitted that she was a witch and that she had cast a spell on Betsy. She told Mrs. Hogan that as long as the tea in the chest was kept airtight, she (Old Susan) would not be able to empty her stomach of the tea that she had drunk since the time Betsy's tea was put in the chest. The witch was wild-eyed and suffering mortal agony. She promised that she would remove the curse from Betsy and never visit a curse on any one again, if only Mrs. Hogan would remove the packing from the keyhole of the chest.

Mrs. Hogan was moved by the woman's suffering, appeals, and promises and she removed the packing. At the instant that the packing was removed, air entered the chest and the witch vomited more than three pints of tea. Betsy became decidedly better at once and was a robust girl in two weeks' time. And true to her word, never again did the witch of Pine Station visit a curse upon anyone in the community.

The witch died several years ago, but Henry and Kittie Stang, now elderly people, still live in Pine and they have in their possession Aunt Sarah's linen chest. Mr. Stang told me this story in late afternoon a few weeks ago, and after finishing he lit a lantern and proudly led me to a dark corner in his barn and showed me a fine old chest, the very one in which the tea had been locked. The chest is about four and a half feet long, two

SARAH AND THE CHILDREN DISCOVER THE OVERTURNED TIERCE OF LARD

feet wide and twenty inches high. It is made of large white pine boards and has hand-made hinges, lock and key hole plate. It is a remaining link which connects the Pine Station of today with the superstitious beliefs of almost three-quarters of a century ago.

(As in previous articles, this story has been written just as it was told to me. Exact places and dates are given, but fictitious names have been substituted for real names, so as to avoid offense to any of the characters or their living relatives).

XII

Just in the Nick of Time

Bark peeling was quite an industry in Clinton County a half century ago [mid 1880's]. There were many small tanneries in the county and each of these tanneries used a considerable quantity of rock oak and hemlock bark in tanning hides. In late years most of the small tanneries have disappeared and have been supplemented by a few large tanneries. The bark peeling industry of Clinton County has fallen off to a great extent for two reasons: (1) there is little hemlock and rock oak remaining to be peeled, and (2) improved methods of tanning hides make it possible to tan a certain amount of leather today with one tenth the amount of tan-bark that was formerly required.

A number of years ago the old lumbermen were in the habit of peeling the bark of the white pine. White pine bark had no commercial value. It was peeled simply because of the fact that the saw often carried the pitch of the pine bark and left a red streak in the clear white pine boards. Today Pennsylvania has few stands of good white pine timber and our lumberman are less particular about sawing this kind of wood. White pine logs are not peeled before being sawed, in Pennsylvania today.

The bark on the oak and the hemlock "loosens up" in the spring of the year and bark peeling usually began early in May and ended about the fourth of July, or by the middle of July. The bark peelers began their work as soon as the bark loosened on the trunks of the oak and hemlock and they worked with feverish haste, and many hours each day, for as many weeks as bark could be peeled. The bark peelers worked for jobbers and were paid a certain amount of money per ton of bark peeled or were paid on the basis of the number of board feet in the logs they had peeled.

Fifty years ago men went to the woods in Clinton County in the spring of the year in twos and threes and fours to batch and peel bark. They built their own shanties and cooked their own meals. These shanties were often built of logs. Some of the shanties were temporary structures, unchinked, and having a door that could be opened and closed but windows that were only empty holes. Some of the shanties were flimsy, being made of a skeleton of logs covered with large sheets of bark. But many of the shanties used by the bark peelers were of more durable construction and were used in winter as well as in the bark peeling season. On nearly any mountain a person could find a bark peeler's shanty.

REPLICA OF A BARK PEELER'S SHANTY

A shanty made in 1973 of hemlock bark. The shanty is located at the Pennsylvania Lumber Museum in Potter County and is similar to the less permanent shanties in which bark peelers lived as they moved from one hemlock grove to the next, in Central Pennsylvania in the late 1800's, when peeling bark for the tanneries.

PEELING THE HEMLOCK BARK

In the late 1800's hemlock trees in Central Pennsylvania were cut mainly for their bark. Forty years ago enormous, decaying hemlock trunks were found scattered on the mountainsides. The trunks had been abandoned after the bark was removed. The tannic acid in the bark was used in the manufacture of leather. Note the large pieces of bark lying on the ground. The inside of the bark was light in color, matching the color of the denuded trunk.

HAULING THE HEMLOCK BARK FROM THE FOREST

Teamsters hauled loads of bark to the tannery or to a railroad siding. The loads were stacked high, for the bark was light in weight.

STACKED HEMLOCK BARK AT A PENNSYLVANIA TANNERY

There were numerous tanneries in Central Pennsylvania from 1875 until 1930. Stacks of this sort were common, adjacent to the tanneries. From a photograph taken in August 1923.

These bark peelers were a happy lot. The lonesomeness of the woods and the monotony of their tasks brought the bark peelers close together and the men in their camps had many a good time—hunting on the side and singing and swapping stories and fishing.

Early in the 1890's three brothers by the names of Bob, George and Jake Anderson were peeling bark in Kammerdiner Hollow. Harry Overdorf, a boy of eleven years, lived with these three men and was their water boy. The Anderson brothers built a little shanty about one quarter mile below the hollow, east of the Kammerdiner farm. The Kammerdiner farm has been deserted for years. Today its location is marked by a small clearing and the ruins of the stone foundation of the house, but all traces of the Anderson shanty have disappeared.

On a warm and bright day late in May the three bark peelers and the water boy were working in the woods about one hundred yards above the shanty. At noon they dropped their spuds and turned to go to the shanty for dinner. They saw a mother bear with cubs. One of the men proposed the idea of stealing a cub from the mother bear. The other bark peelers fell

TOO CLOSE FOR COMFORT

in with the idea at once. It was decided that Bob, being the longest legged of the three men, and the fastest runner, should grab a cub and run for the shanty while the other two men would run between the mother bear and the shanty and stave her off by brandishing pine knots until Bob would have the cub safely in-doors. All three of the bark peelers were plucky and they dashed into the scheme at once, while the water boy looked on with shining eyes. There was going to be some fun. And he wasn't going to miss it, not for a good bit. A bear cub wasn't caught every day!

Bob made a dash for the cub that was farthest away from the mother bear. He picked the cub up and put it in his arms and sped towards the shanty. A full grown bear is a clumsy looking and squint-eyed animal but it did not require much time for this mother bear to take in the situation and to act. The mother instinct in the bear is very strong. The mother emitted a bellow and broke out in a run to retrieve her stolen off-spring and to punish the "bear-napper."

Bob had a handicap of only a few yards. The bear gained speed with every step and her bellow grew louder as she pursued the one who stole her cub. The other two men, George and Jake, became thoroughly scared. They dropped their pine knots and hid behind large white pine stumps. From their haven of refuge they called to Bob: "Leg 'er Bob," "She's gainin' on you, Bob," "More speed, Bob," and so on, all of which helped Bob very little. Bob was approaching the shanty, but so was the bear, and only a half step in the rear. Just as Bob got to the shanty he tossed the cub out of his arms to its mother and dashed in the cabin and bolted the door. The mother bear made no more fuss. She was satisfied. She had her cub. Bob was satisfied, too. He was behind a securely fastened door. The bear had been ready to seize Bob. One more step to go and the bear would have had Bob. His presence of mind which prompted him to throw the cub to its mother was the only thing that saved Bob. And the enthusiastic cheers of "You made 'er, Bob," from behind the pine stumps, probably did not sound nearly as good to Bob as the slamming of the door, the click of the latch and the sliding of the bolt.

XIII

The Witch of Werner's Mill

Sugar Valley was settled late in the 1700's. The Hessian soldiers who fought in the Revolutionary War were among the first of these settlers. Many Pennsylvania Germans moved into the valley in succeeding years. The settlers turned to farming and to the making of maple sugar. Sugar Valley to this day has remained, for the most part, a prosperous Pennsylvania German farming section but the maple sugar business has greatly decreased due to the disappearance of many of the fine groves of sugar maple trees.

The Sugar Valley people were very superstitious a half century ago. They feared certain people whom they considered to be witches and they pointed to dilapidated houses and told of nightly pilgrimages of white and bony figures to these buildings. The Valley was so much steeped in superstition that it was not very difficult for a person with some degree of imagination or fear to "see" spooks or "suspect" some one of being a witch. "Suspicions" and "scenes" were eagerly spread from mouth to mouth and the scenes and suspicions probably grew with each telling, until finally some well-rounded and fanciful hair-raising stories circulated, which formed the center of discussion by many a fireside, and in many a nightly gathering at "the general store." The spook and witch stories were common and prove interesting to this day. An aged lifelong resident of Tylersville, now eighty-eight years old, said a few weeks ago, "When I was a boy every fence post in Sugar Valley was 'spooked'."

The Sugar Valley people believed that a woman who was a witch and who possessed super-natural powers could change herself into the form of various animals. They also believed that if a person would shoot or strike the witch while she was promenading in the form of an animal the witch would suffer the effects of the shot or the blow when she returned to her natural form, unless the shot or blow would kill her while she was travelling in the guise of a cat or dog or some other animal. It was also believed that the shooting of a certain kind of bullet into the object that the sorceress had bewitched would result in the wounding or the death of the sorceress. The following story of the Witch of Werner's Mill, in Tylersville, is one of many of the Sugar Valley witch stories that are almost similar to it.

Ezra Hopple, of Tylersville, was a shrewd man. For some time there had been strange happenings in Tylersville. People spoke of witches and shook their heads solemnly. And the grist mill in the town was said to be "haunted." Ezra pondered the situation.

FRONT VIEW OF LOGANTON FLOUR AND FEED MILL, SIMILAR TO NEARBY "WERNER'S MILL"

Built in 1824 by A. Kleckner this Loganton mill was later owned by Dan Morris, and still later by William Meyer and E. E. Meyer and Sons. The mill is fifty-five feet by sixty feet and was built with white pine timber eighteen inches high, seventeen inches wide, and sixty feet long.

John Werner was the local miller. Business was good in those days early in the 1870's. His grist mill was in operation day and night. Werner ran his mill during the day and employed a man to operate the mill at night. Werner had difficulty keeping a night man in his employ. In one, two or three nights, or in a week at the most, a new man would leave, and always with some weird tale of spooks in the mill.

Ezra Hopple wanted to get to the bottom of matters. He had some suspicions as to who or what was at the bottom of these peculiar happenings in Tylersville. In about the year 1872, when Ezra was approximately forty years old, he went to John Werner and asked for a job. The night man had quit that morning and Ezra offered his services. The miller said to Mr. Hopple, "You can't run that mill." Hopple replied, "Yes I can." Many men had failed Werner and had quit the job soon after accepting it. Werner discounted the boasting of new and untried applicants. After a bit of hesitation Werner agreed to employ Ezra Hopple as night miller.

Ezra began his duties that very evening. He worked all night, never stopping to sleep or even to take a short nap on a bag of feed. Soon after dark he saw a black cat walking through the mill. He could not see where the cat came from or where it went. It appeared at an unexpected time and disappeared mysteriously. But Ezra went on about his duties and tried to appear unconcerned. He remained on guard and was alert all through the night, hoping to let nothing pass unseen in the mill.

Nothing out of the ordinary, except the appearance of the black cat, occurred the first night. During the following day Ezra recounted to himself the stories he had heard about the mill and tried to fit those stories in with his observations at the mill, of the previous night.

When Ezra Hopple went to work the second night he had different plans. Frequently in those days flour was ground during the day time and chop was ground at night. Grist mills were run by water-power, and burr mills, rather than roller mills, were used. Flour and chop were ground between two large round mill stones lying on top of each other and revolving in opposite directions. The burr mills ground flour and chop much as two stove lids, lying on top of each other and revolving in opposite directions, would grind saltines lying between the lids. The modern roller mills grind flour and chop between sets of rollers, much as a wash wringer wrings clothes. Most of the old burr mills driven by water-power have been supplanted by steam or electric driven roller mills. On that second night at the mill Ezra's work went well. He soon had the burr mills adjusted and the hoppers filled. Everything was running smoothly. He was probably grinding chop.

The old grist mills had a separate little room on the first floor called an "office." The night's work was fairly well under way and so Ezra thought he would go to the office and lie down on the comfortable couch in that room. He took a hatchet and laid it on the couch beside him. He feigned sleep. He had several hunches and he thought it wise to "play 'possum." He had not been lying on the couch very long until he heard muffled footsteps. They came closer and closer. He recognized them to the footfalls of a large cat. The visitor entered the office. It approached Ezra's couch. Ezra recognized the cat to be the same one that had visited him the night before. The cat came up to the side of the couch and raised up on its hind feet, facing the man who appeared to be sleeping. The cat seemed to grow in size as it raised up before Ezra. After the cat straightened up completely

EZRA HOPPLE SEES A BLACK CAT THE FIRST NIGHT

ON THE SECOND NIGHT EZRA HOPPLE STRIKES AT THE CAT'S PAW

it raised its left paw and was about to strike Ezra Hopple. Hopple had observed every movement and now quickly raised up, seized the hatchet, and struck the cat's paw. He was successful in striking the cat and he cut the last three toes on the black cat's front left foot. The black cat disappeared immediately and Ezra did not see the cat or any other peculiar visitors or antics during the remainder of that night.

In the morning when Ezra saw John Werner, the proprietor of the mill, he said, "I want to see your wife." Werner replied, "You can't see her." Hopple was not one to be set aside. He stated firmly, "Well, I'm going to see her." Werner told him that his wife was sick but Hopple strode on towards the miller's house. Hopple met the miller's daughter and he greeted her by saying, "I want to see your mother." The young Miss Werner said, "No, you can't see her; she isn't out of bed yet." Hopple simply said, "Well I will see her," and he walked into Mrs. Werner's bedroom and saw her privately. Mrs. Werner was a sick woman, and a worried woman that morning. The last three fingers, the small finger, ring finger and thimble finger of her left hand were cut and bandaged. One look at her was sufficient. Ezra Hopple said, "As I thought, you are the

"YOU ARE THE WITCH"

witch who has been causing all this trouble." Mrs. Werner pleaded pathetically with Ezra, asking him never to tell a soul, not even her husband. The witch was caught at last. Ezra's work at the mill was completed and Werner's Mill was never bothered again.

Footnote: Fictitious names have been given to the characters in this story. The person to whom I have given the name Ezra Hopple was born in 1832 and died in 1917, and lies buried in the cemetery beside Mount Zion Church, in Crawford Township, Clinton County. The story was told to me recently by a friend of the deceased person. Because of the lapse of years since the main character's death the exact location of the mill, and the name of the miller have seemed to slip into oblivion. I have given Tylersville as the location and Werner as the name of the miller, knowing only that the scene was laid in "Sugar Valley."

XIV

The Story of Baldwin's Wolf

Two centuries ago Pennsylvania was almost completely covered with dense forests of very valuable timber. All of the state except a few natural meadows and a few rough mountain tops was a dense virgin forest. The timber in this forest was of the very best and could not be surpassed in value by any stands of timber in any parts of the eastern United States. Our forests were filled with many kinds of "big game," such as buffaloes, panthers and wolves. Today virgin timber, buffaloes, panthers and wolves are only a memory in Pennsylvania. They have faded out of reality long ago. The buffaloes disappeared first, then much of the virgin timber, the panthers and the wolves receded. A part of the great stands of timber and the wolves were the last to go.

In the 1700's and the early part of the 1800's many wolves roamed the Clinton County mountains. The State of Pennsylvania paid a bounty on wolves for a number of years. In the 1850's the people of Sugar Valley frequently heard the wolves in packs howling from the mountain tops. By the latter part of the 1870's the wolves of our County and State had been almost completely wiped out. The wasteful cutting of timber and the increase of population did not make for the propagation of this species of wild life.

The wolves of Clinton County killed many sheep and created quite a disturbance at night. Their plaintive wailing from the distant mountain sides and mountain tops struck terror into many a heart. The wolves travelled in small packs and on regular trails. The old lumbermen still call one particular gulch in Wayne Township "Wolf Hollow" for the wolves travelled through this gulch regularly on their pilgrimages. Wolf Hollow lies between Henry Run and the Pine-Loganton Road, two and a half miles south of Pine, and is about a quarter of a mile north of a small spring along the Pine-Loganton Road, that is called "Gum Spring." When the wolves travelled through Wolf Hollow and along Henry Run they were probably travelling between White Deer Valley and McElhattan on a fairly regular schedule, just as the Indians moved from valley to valley on quite definite schedules and trails.

Today Wolf Hollow is only a name, only a memory of days of yore. Shortly after the Civil War there was real timber along Henry Run and in Wolf Hollow and the wolves travelled that section frequently. Mr. Harry

Baldwin was then a young man. He had fought in the Civil War three and a half years on the side of the Union and returned to his home at the end of the war. He married almost at once, left his wife in Avis [a village in Clinton County] and set out for the Wolf Hollow section. He bought twenty-three acres of timber, hired a man, built a cabin and began cutting timber in summer, fall and winter and rafting it to Marietta in spring. In the fall of 1866 he and his hired man built a shanty of white pine logs on a little flat, between two large hemlock trees, on the Wolf Hollow side of Henry Run, at the spring which forms the source of Henry Run. This spot is scarcely a mile and a half south of Wolf Hollow, and it was directly on the old Wolf trail. Baldwin and his helper chinked their cabin with moss that they gathered from the bed of the stream, and they shaved shingles for the roof from white pine billets. The cabin was rectangular, about ten feet by fourteen feet. The side walls were about seven feet high and the roof was gabled. There was only one window and one door. The window was cut in one of the side walls and the door in the other side wall. The ends of the cabin had no openings.

THE WOLVES BECAME BOLD

Baldwin and his helper were snug in their shanty. They were nestled among the mighty white pines and had a stout and cozy home. They cut the mighty white pines and hewed out square timber fifty and sixty feet long. Baldwin dreamed of cutting and squaring up thousands of feet of white pine that winter, and dreamed of floating it down Henry Run to the river in the spring freshets, with the aid of splash dams, and then rafting it down the Susquehanna to Marietta, below Harrisburg, and there selling his fine timber, the product of his winter's labor, to the great lumber merchants who gathered in Marietta to meet the raftsmen and bargain with them for their valuable rafts.

As cold weather came on, Baldwin and his helper became aware of the fact that wolves travelled past their shanty frequently. When the snows came and when the winter grew more severe the wolves became hungrier, howled louder and became bolder. Baldwin brought some hams to his shanty, to serve as a part of the supply of meat for the winter and he hung these hams on the rafters of his shanty, up in the gable directly under the roof. The wolves smelled the ham, sniffed eagerly and howled hungrily from a safe distance. Night after night they came closer to the cabin. Soon they gained enough temerity to jump on the cabin roof late at night and tear the shingles off the roof with their claws. This action was repeated several nights. The wolves came in packs varying in number from three and four to seven and eight. It was time to do something. The wolves were ravenous and were growing bolder each night. Soon they might tear a large enough hole in the roof so as to be able to crawl into the shanty.

Baldwin had an old flint lock muzzle loader. He had heard that if a wolf was shot it would charge forward savagely in the direction it was looking when it was shot, and use its dying strength to attack anything that it encountered in this mad rush. In making such a lunge wolves probably felt instinctively that they were rushing at their attackers and would be able to wreak vengeance. At any rate the old wolf hunters took caution and tried to get a broadside shot at wolves, rather than a head-on shot. Baldwin decided that the wolves must be killed off, or at least frightened.

It was night, and late in December in the year 1866. There was snow on the ground and several wolves were howling up on the hill towards the Pine Road. They were reconnoitering to gather courage to descend the hill and pounce upon the cabin roof. Baldwin loaded his gun with powder, paper wadding and a solid lead ball. He opened the window and the door of his cabin and placed meat on the window sill for bait. His bed was directly under the window. Baldwin went outside of the cabin and laid in wait with his gun, watching the window by peeping into the room through the doorway. He did not need to wait very long. The wolves smelled the fresh meat and a pack of them drew closer. They came to a place that was within a little more than a hundred yards of the shanty. One wolf, apparently the leader of the small band, approached still closer. This old denisen of the forest advanced and advanced until he was within an easy stone throw of the shanty. He stopped. He perked up his ears more rigidly and warily than previously. He was becoming very cautious. Yet, there was a hungry, yes, a ravenous, gleam in his eyes. His greed for meat became stronger than his sense of fear and his capacity for caution. He loped up easily to the window, stopping only a few times and then grasped the meat from the window sill with one swift motion of his savage looking jaws and long cruel teeth. Just as the wolf sprang upon the bait Baldwin fired.

THE DYING WOLF TORE THE BLANKETS TO SHREDS

The ball was well directed. The wolf was facing the marksman and the ball entered the wolf's head. The shot was mortal. The wolf had only a few minutes to live but he still had a great deal of "fight" left in him. He lunged forward to make his dying attack on the person who had shot him. The wolf fell through the window and landed on the bed. The wolf went no further. He tore the blankets to shreds and demolished the bed and then died. When he came in contact with the bed he was probably crazed and blinded and he may have thought that the woolen blankets were the clothing on the body of the man who shot him. At any rate the wolf battled the bed and not Baldwin. The wolf died on the bed in his struggle.

Baldwin had shot one wolf. The wolves were still giving him trouble; but, rather than lose any more beds and bedding he decided to trap wolves instead of shooting them. He never shot another wolf but he forged traps from iron and "set" for wolves for many years. He was never successful in trapping wolves, however. He killed but one wolf in his lifetime.

Baldwin continued to cut pine and raft it to Marietta year after year. Gradually the wolves disappeared from Wayne Township and from all of Clinton County and Pennsylvania. The fine old white pines disappeared also. Fewer rafts went dow the river each year. And the old time woodsmen, of Baldwin's stamp, disappeared also. Only a few remain today. And they are real men. Go out and talk to them. They will tell you great stories of "the good old days." These few remaining mountaineer woodsmen of the old school are a fine type of real manhood.

Footnote: As nearly as possible exact places and dates are given in this article but the name of the chief character, Harry Baldwin, is fictitious. The man to whom I have given the name Baldwin "lumbered" in Wayne Township for many years and died in about the year 1905. He was buried in Quiggle Cemetery, Wayne Township, along the Susquehanna River at the southern abutment of the New York Central Railroad bridge, which is about halfway between Pine Station and McElhattan. About a year ago one of Baldwin's oldest sons, who is still living, gave me a large powder horn that his father, Harry Baldwin, used for years. This powder horn is probably the same one that Baldwin used on that cold night in December, 1866, when he shot the wolf on Henry Run.

XV

The Hex Doctor and the Witch of Farrandsville

Farrandsville, on the West Branch of the Susquehanna River, six miles above Lock Haven, has an interesting history. It has been a "ghost town" for more than a century. Founded in the winter of 1831-1832 in the wilderness by William P. Farrand of Philadelphia for a group of Boston capitalists, it soon had a furnace for the manufacture of iron and a nail mill. Many of the inhabitants of the new town worked in bituminous coal mines adjacent to Farrandsville. The mines were connected with the town by a railroad. A steamboat carried passengers and freight between Farrandsville and Lock Haven.

In 1835 the nail mill was capable of manufacturing ten tons of nails daily and a furnace had turned out nearly 300 tons of castings in the preceding six months. Three veins of coal had been opened and a rolling mill and a large hotel were being erected. (Sherman Day, *Historical Collections of the State of Pennsylvania,* 1843, page 240).

The coal veins were thin and the transportation to market was difficult. Having been founded during a period of speculative frenzy in the United States, the town soon withered. In 1847 agents of the Queen of Spain bought the town and surrounding tracts of land. Two magnificent buildings were erected near Farrandsville for the Queen, a hotel, destroyed by fire in 1892, and an elaborate mansion that was in use until 1910.

The mansion was four stories in height and had a porch in front with four tall, round columns. The large lock and the heavy key for the main door of the mansion finally found their way into the collections of the Clinton County Historical Society.

At the turn of the century a legend surrounded the mansion, as follows. During a period when a bar was operated in the basement there were frequent disputes between patrons who sometimes settled their differences by the use of firearms. There were holes, resembling bullet holes, in the doors. A man was killed in a duel and his body was hidden under the floor.

Whether or not there was any truth in the legend, Farrandsville and immediate vicinity was for decades only a "ghost" of its original activity and splendor. Efforts to develop industry at Farrandsville, first with Boston

CHARCOAL IRON FURNACE AT FARRANDSVILLE

The furnace was unsuccessful, partly because of the poor quality of local iron ore and the difficulty in transporting the finished product to market. The furnace is approximately thirty feet high. In 1974 it continues to be a beautiful piece of masonry and one of the best preserved charcoal iron furnaces in Pennsylvania.

QUEEN OF SPAIN'S MANSION NEAR FARRANDSVILLE
Many residents of Clinton County believed the building was erected as a place of refuge for Queen Isabella II of Spain at a time that Spanish politics were particularly turbulent.

capital and later with the Queen's money, were unsuccessful and the land was sold for taxes. Later a fire brick plant was established at Farrandsville but in early twentieth century it was abandoned for a number of years.°

In a locality with a "ghost town" background, such as that of Farrandsville, it was not difficult for a witch story to thrive in late nineteenth century.

Fifty and sixty years ago [about 1875] many sections of Clinton County were steeped in superstition. Weird stories concerning ghosts and witches were whispered from mouth to mouth. Ghost stories can be dug up in all parts of the county. Pine Station and Sugar Valley had their witches as we

° The large tracts of land that had been owned by the Boston group and then by the Queen of Spain were purchased by the Commonwealth of Pennsylvania. In 1974 State game lands surround Farrandsville and a State forest adjoins the game lands.

saw in earlier articles of this series. Other sections of the county also had their witches. Farrandsville did not escape the touch of the supernatural.

Two very odd characters lived near Farrandsville fifty years ago; the one, John Applegate, a man of about sixty-five years, the other, Sal Kervine, a wizened and bent woman in her eighties. Each of these people lived by themselves about five miles apart, the one a widower, the other a spinster. Both of these people were very eccentric. Applegate pow-wowed and was known as a "hex doctor." Sal Kervine lived in a lonesome spot and her life seemed to be shrouded in mystery. Few people, if any, could get to know her. Because of her aloofness and peculiar ways she had long been called a witch.

Sal Kervine lived in a log house by the side of an old lumber road. There was a fine spring of water near her house. The teamsters frequently halted their lumber wagons in front of her spring and took time to drink their fill of good fresh sparkling water. Sal was the type of person who could take offense and hold a grudge. And she was accused of laying a curse on or bewitching people against whom she held a grievance. On several occasions teamsters found that after stopping their wagons at the spring they would have a great deal of difficulty in starting out with their teams again. It seemed as though the wagons were bolted to the ground. The horses would pull and strain and tug, yet the wagons would not budge an inch. This sort of thing happened several times in the course of a few months.

A teamster by the name of Tom Stewart stopped at the spring for water daily. He hauled logs on scheduled time, making three trips a day to the railroad station. One day Stewart had a quarrel over a small matter with Sal and she had given him glaring looks every time that he saw her since the day of the dispute. One day about two months after the dispute took place Stewart was driving down the road on his second trip for that day. He was about a half hour late but he was thirsty so he took time to stop for a good drink of water. He got his drink, sprang up on the wagon and gave his horses a crisp "Giddap." The horses strained at their bits. They pulled hard on the butt chains. The harness creaked but the wagon did not move. Stewart was in a hurry. He was late. The boss would be waiting for him. He raised his whip and used it lightly on each horse. The coal-black three thousand pound team tugged and pulled and strained harder than before. Stewart's horses were not failing him. They were putting every ounce of their strength into the task at hand; they were doing their best to move that wagon. Something was holding the wagon. Stewart realized that his team was doing its best. In an instant he saw the situation—"The witch, 'Old Sal,' yes sir-e-e-e," he muttered between clenched teeth. Stewart picked up his axe, jumped off the wagon and with one blow of the axe he broke a spoke in the front wheel. He jumped back on the wagon and

TOM STEWART BREAKING THE "SPELL"

called to his horses. This time the wagon moved freely.

Stewart chuckled to himself as he rode to the station. The next day he stopped to see "Old Sal." He did not see her out of doors so he went to her house. He found she had a broken arm. "Just as I thought," he mused to himself and went back to his team. No wagon was ever held up at the spring after that.

John Applegate, "hex doctor," lumberman and farmer, was an interesting character. Some people feared him but most of his neighbors liked him. In those days, fifty years ago, Applegate and all of his neighbors who had cows turned their cattle loose to graze in the woods. Good pastures were none too plentiful in the mountains and custom sanctioned the practice of turning the stock out to browse on whatever it could find. With the aid of cow bells the matter of corralling the cattle was not such a difficult job, but once in a great while a man might lose a cow.

One summer Applegate and his two nearest neighbors lost every head of cattle they owned, twenty-four cows, all told. Eight of the cows belonged to Applegate, seven to Wells and nine to Brown, the two neighbors. All of the twenty-four cows disappeared on the same day. Applegate, Wells and Brown failed to locate their cattle one evening. The three men searched together for three days and nights for the missing cows. They could not find a trace of their stock, not even as much as the distant tinkle of a cow bell.

The three men returned to Applegate's house, tired and worn, shortly after dark on the third day. Brown hastened on to his own home but Applegate persuaded Wells to stay with him for the night, promising Wells that if he would stay for the night the cows would be there in the morning. Applegate told his guest that he was tired of hunting for the cattle. "Just wait until morning and I'll see that our cows come back without us doing any more wildgoose chasing," he said to Wells, shaking his head significantly and winking one eye slowly.

After he had supper Wells was shown his bed and he retired. The next morning he awoke early and looked out of his bedroom window. He looked out just in time to see some strange happenings. He saw his host, John Applegate, coming out of the front door with a large Bible and a pair of scissors. Applegate walked to the corner of the house, opened the Bible and read a chapter. Then he placed the scissors on the Bible and closed the Holy Book so that the scissors laid in the middle of the closed book. The "hex doctor" saw to it that the scissors were opened (forming an X) when he placed them in the Bible. Applegate then put the Good Book on a log and waited. He appeared to be anxious about something. He paced to and fro and scanned the edge of the clearing with his eyes. Wells was at a loss to know what such an odd performance meant, yet Wells took in the entire scene from his window.

Wells noticed that about fifteen minutes after Applegate laid down his Bible with the scissors in it the old "hex doctor" became excited and glanced eagerly from one side of the clearing to the other side. He stood erect and tense and seemed to be straining eyes and ears. Something was in the air! What would happen next? Wells, in his bedroom, became just as excited as his host who was in the front yard. The suspense was not of great duration. A few seconds after Applegate became tense, taut and rigid there was a faint tinkling of cow bells and within a few more seconds

MR. APPLEGATE SETS THE "HEX"

the bells could be heard very plainly. Cows came dashing into the clearing from the woods. They came from all directions. They came at "full tilt" with tails straight up in the air and bells clanging loudly. They charged for the barnyard. They could not all get through the barnyard gate at once so some of them, in their haste, jumped over the barnyard fence. Applegate quietly walked up to the barnyard, closed the gate, and counted the stock. Twenty-four cows! Not a cow missing. Applegate, Wells and Brown each regained every cow they had lost.

APPLEGATE'S ASTONISHING VICTORY

The scene from the bedroom window astonished and disturbed Wells. He concluded that the "hex doctor" had tired of hunting for the cows after search for three days and nights and had decided to send the "Evil Spirit" out to find the cattle and drive them home. Wells never went back again to sleep in Applegate's house.

XVI

Old-Time Ballads and Folk Songs of Clinton County

The people of Old England entertained themselves by singing numerous folk songs. These ballads were stories told in song. The ballads concerned every day happenings, local customs, and dreams and aspirations of the plain rural folk. These songs were passed on orally for several centuries. Many originated probably as early as the 1300's and were widely sung in Shakespeare's time, in the 1500's. Folk songs were popular in Europe as well as in England. The pioneers who settled in Clinton County and in other parts of North Central Pennsylvania were mainly of English, Scotch-Irish, Huguenot, and German origin. They brought with them many of the folk songs of their native lands. They lived a somewhat isolated life in the Pennsylvania wilderness and for entertainment they turned to music and story telling.

The early generations of Pennsylvania mountaineers were poets and musicians, more so than the present generation. On long winter evenings there was music in their farmhouses, cabins and lumber camps and there were old-timers by the fireplace to tell thrilling war, Indian, ghost, witch, bear, panther or elk stories. In later years when bark was peeled, crews of bark-peelers assembled beside a stream or under a tree on summer evenings to listen to the songster of the crowd sing his favorites while the camp musicians played their instruments. Until about thirty-five years ago no lumber camp in the Black Forest, north of Lock Haven, was complete unless it contained musical instruments. The favorite instruments of Clinton County were the violin and the mouth organ. There were also quite a number of accordions and a few harps and dulcimers. The dulcimer was a musical instrument with wire strings. The strings were struck with light hammers. Dulcimers are now very scarce in North Central Pennsylvania.

Many ot the mountaineers were skilled in playing these instruments and others were skilled in composing and singing. Quite a few of the old folk songs of England and Europe, in slightly changed form, were sung in the Clinton County mountains and many new ones concerning life in the lumber camps and on the canals, and concerning other topics of common interest were composed here in our mountains. Many of these ballads were light and airy while some were of a philosophical nature. Some of these songs were crude, being merely chants. Others were lonesome crooning tunes while still others had a rollicking swing that was almost classical. These folk songs were passed down from mouth to mouth during the past one hundred years. They were sung by thewomen in many of the homes as well as by the men in the lumber camps and on the canal boats. A few men gained outstanding recognition as ballad singers and their fame spread for miles, especially in the West Branch Valley of the Susquehanna. Most of the great old singers and composers have passed on and some of the best of these folk songs have disappeared and have been forgotten, just as many of the fascinating old English folk songs have disappeared. Fortunately, however, some of these fine old ballads of the Pennsylvania Highlands have been preserved through the efforts of Colonel Henry W. Shoemaker, of McElhattan. In 1919 he published a compilation of old folk songs that were formerly sung in Clinton, Potter and adjoining counties. These songs appeared in book form under the title *North Pennsylvania Minstrelsy*.

The following are a few of the old songs that were popular in Clinton County a generation or more ago. These five ballads have been taken from the Shoemaker collection.

I. The Jolly Lumbermen

This ballad was sung by Leary Miller, Lick Run, Clinton County, and was collected by Colonel Shoemaker in January of 1901. In the seventies, eighties and nineties, Lock Haven was a great center for employing lumber jacks. The men went to work in the woods late in the fall and lumbered until spring. Once employed they were expected to stay on the job until the end of the season. Sometimes men deserted camp during the winter, leaving their employers in a lurch. Sometimes such desertions were justified for occasionally a boss did not live up to agreements concerning food, living quarters, hours and wages. This ballad, The Jolly Lumbermen, was popular with raftsmen on the West Branch of the Susquehanna.

Come, all you jolly lumbermen,
And listen to my song;
But do not get uneasy,
For I won't detain you long.
Concerning some jolly lumbermen
Who once agreed to go
And spend a winter recently
On Colley's Run, i-oh!

We landed in Lock Haven
    The year of seventy-three.
A minister of the Gospel
    One evening said to me,
Are you the party of lumbermen
    That once agreed to go
And spend a winter pleasantly
    On Colley's Run, i-oh!

Oh, yes, we'll go to Colley's Run,
    To that we will agree,
Provided you pay good wages,
    Our passage to and fro.
Then we'll agree to accompany you
    On Colley's Run, i-oh!

Oh, yes, we'll pay good wages,
    Your passage to and fro,
Provided you will sign papers
    To stay the winter through.
But, mind you, if you get homesick
    And back you swear you'll go.
You'll have to pay your own passage down
    From Colley's Run, i-oh!

'Twas by that tarnal agreement
    That we agreed to go,
Full five and twenty in number,
    All able-bodied men.
The road, it was a pleasant one,
    By tail we had to go,
Till we landed at McFarling's tavern,
    Full seventeen miles below.

But there our joys were ended,
    Our troubles, they began.
The captain and the foreman
    Came following up the run
They led us in every direction,
    Through some places I did not know,
Among the pines which grew so tall
    On Colley's Run, i-oh!

Our hearts were clad with iron,
Our soles were shod with steel,
But the usages of that winter
Would scarcely make a shield.
For our grub the dogs would laugh at,
And our beds were wet with snow;
God grant there is no worse place on earth
Than Colley's Run, i-oh!

But now the spring has come again,
And the ice-bound streams are free.
We'll float our logs to Williamsport,
Our friends we'll haste to see.
Our sweethearts, they will welcome us
And bid others not to go
To that God-forsaken gehooley of a place,
Of Colley's Run, i-oh!

"THE RITES OF SPRING"

II. All Is Vanity, Saith The Preacher

This folk song was sung by John Q. Dyce, of McElhattan, in 1900 and was collected by Colonel Shoemaker. John Q. Dyce was a famed poet, composer, singer, raftsman and story teller of the West Branch Valley. He was born in 1830 and died thirty years ago, in 1904. Some of his entertaining "tall" stories still live on and a number of the ballads that he composed and sung are preserved in the Shoemaker Collection.

Many of the early lumbermen in Clinton County, and other places, were a bit rough as to habits of living. But nearly all of them were jovial good fellows, ready to be a true friend to almost any one at almost any time. And such is one of the greatest tests of true character. Many of the lumbermen were away in the woods far from the sound of church bells. Perhaps many of them did not care to sit still for an hour and listen to a sermon. At any rate the attempt to bring the gospel to the men at Sinnemahoning may not have been successful. Here is the story as Dyce gave it in song:

There is a place called Sinnemahone,
Of which but little good is known:
For sinning, ill must be its fame,
Since Sin begins its very name.
That people think they should begin
To drop the useless word Mahone,
And call the country simply, SIN!
But to my tale—some years agone
The Presbytery—having heard
Of the sad state of Sin—resolved
To send some one to preach the Word,
And Mr. Thompson was bid to see then

To the conversion of the heathen.
I shall not linger long to tell
Of all that on the way befell;
How he was lost among the bushes,
And floundered through the reeds and rushes;
To corn-cobs fried in 'possum fat!
How his black coat's unusual hue
Caused a grim hunter to pursue
And cock his gun to blow him through,
Believing, as I've heard him swear,
Our missionary was a bear.
"'Tis true," he said, "I never counted
On seeing such a thing as a bear
Upon a good stout pony mounted;
But yet I can with safety swear
That such a very wondrous sight
We might expect by day or night,
Rather than, in our hills, to note
A parson with a rale black coat."
The news soon spread around the land.
That parson Thompson, on next Sunday,
Would in the schoolhouse take his stand,
And preach to them at least for one day.
The Sunday came, and with it came
All of the ragged population;
Men, women, children, dogs, to hear
The tidings of salvation.
The women came in linsey-woolsey,
And tall, wool hats increased their stature;
The men in shirts and leather leggins;
The brats and dogs in dress of nature!
The men who seldom stop at trifles
Brought tomahawks and knives and rifles,
Service began—the parson wondered
To hear the singing that they made.

BILLY TENCH, UNWILLING LISTENER

Some "Yankee Doodle"—some "Old Hundred"—
The hounds, astonished, howled and thund'red,
Until the forest shook with dread.
The singing o'er, the prayer was said,
But scarcely had the text been read,
When, panting with fatigue and fear,
Rushed past the door a hunted deer.
And for the sermon mattered not;
Forth dashed the dogs—not one was mute—
Men, women, children followed suit.
The men prepared the deer to slaughter,
The girls to head it to the water.
None stayed but lame old Billy Tench,
Who sat unwilling on his bench.
Not for the sake of hymn or prayer,
Did Billy keep his station there,
But, as he said, with rueful phiz—
"For an awful spell of roomatiz!"
The parson groaned with inward pain,
And lifting up his hands amain,
Cried, dolefully, "'Tis all in vain!"
Up starting numbly from his bench,
"'Tis not in vain," cried Billy Tench,
"When my good hound, old Never-Fail,
Once gets his nose upon the trail,
There's not a spike buck anywhere,
Can get away from him, I'll swear.

III. An Old Timer's Plaint

Some of the old lumbermen must have been philosophers. They must have spent some time with their chins in their hands, wondering what life was all about, and questioning Franklin's adage, "Early to bed and early to rise makes a man healthy, wealthy and wise," and the belief that is so often taught, that one gets out of life just what he puts into it.

The following ballad and a snatch of another, printed directly below it in these columns take this happy-go-lucky or cynical, whichever it may be, philosophy of life. The first "An Old Timer's Plaint," was sung by Gid Martin in about the year 1900 and was collected by John C. French, one of Colonel Shoemaker's collaborators. It was a song of the Black Forest lumber camps.

Some folks say there's no such
thing as good or evil luck;
Success depends on labor backed
by energy and pluck—

Just put your shoulder to the
wheel and lift with all your might,
From early in the morning till
stars come out at night!
They may be right; but—

For fifty years I've buckled down
and nearly broke my back
A-tugging; still that pesky wheel
is sticking in the track!
I haven't got it moved an inch from
where it first was stuck;
The more I lift, the deeper down
it settles in the muck!
My kind of luck; yet—

I have a friend who never works—
I see him every day:
He's neatly dressed, and always
seems contented, blythe and gay.
He's always talking politics—be-
lieves in standing pat—
He's quite a fan, and always knows
when Baker comes to bat.
Now, think of that! Well—

You never can make me believe it
all depends on work!
Success, sometimes, will pounce
upon the consummated shirk;

And so I'm taking little stock in
all the silly truck
About the tugging at the wheel—
the wheel that's always stuck!
I know it's luck! Yes, sir!

IV. Tramping Chant

This fragment brings out the philosophy of the wandering lumber jack and probably comes to us from Potter County.

Oh! the firefly is brilliant,
But he hasn't any mind;
He wanders through creation
With his headlight on behind.

Refrain—

Then cast your bread upon the water,
And you'll see just what returns,
Another time—oh, well, no matter;
He who travels, sometimes learns.

V. Kate Maury

And here is an amusing little ditty that was popular in the West Branch Valley. It was sung by a stonecutter in Wayne Township (neighborhood of Pine Station and McElhattan) about 1857. It was collected by John H. Chatham, a native of McElhattan and an old raftsman, teacher, naturalist-poet and sage, who aided Colonel Shoemaker in collecting folk songs.

Young men, draw near unto me,
And listen to my story.
I'll tell you of a plan I took
To fool Miss Kate Maury.

And if she would go with me
Down into yonder bower,
"And if your father won't come by
We'll spend a happy hour."

I did not have to ask her twice,
She put on her best bonnet.
My heart was beating very fast,
As 'cross the fields we ran it.

"It's now we're here alone,
And no one knows the matter.
It's you must die or else comply,
For I've no time to flatter."

Kate seemed quite pleased, my
hand she squeezed.
"There's but one thing I fear, sir;
Is that my father may come this way,
And he would find us here, sir.

"But if you'll climb the highest tree
That rises in this bower,
And if my father keeps away,
We'll spend the happy hour."

Kate stood at the foot of the tree
Until I had ascended:
"It's you may get down the way you got up,
For now your fun is ended.

"You look just like an owl," she said;
"Your company I shun, sir.
You may eat your plums and suck the stones,
For I am going to run, sir."

Away Kate heeled it over the plain,
And left me here distracted,
I ripped, I swore, my shirt I tore,
To think how I had acted.

But when I came to think it o'er,
How cunning she had fooled me,
I took fair Katie for my wife,
And ever since she's ruled me.

My song grows tough, I've sung enough
I've nothing more worth rhyming,
But every time Kate smiles on me,
She makes me think of climbing.

KATE MAURY SAYING "GOOD-BYE"

Many other ballads besides these five were sung in Clinton County by hearty pioneers and their descendants during the past one hundred years. The songs printed in the old school books of our county are also interesting. And a number of pieces that are still familiar today and that were not originated in Clinton County were sung frequently; such as "Arkansas Traveller," "Listen to the Mocking Bird," "Old Dan Tucker" and "Old Zep Coon." Let us look for old forgotten ballads that were sung by the sturdy pioneers of our county. We will be glad to get a clue as to the whereabouts of old songs of Clinton County. If you have a clue as to where some old songs can be found drop a penny post card to "Clinton County Weekly," Lock Haven, Pa., and we will be on the job to hunt up the clue for you.

XVII

Horn's Fort

Along the Pennsylvania Railroad near Pine Station there stands a stone bearing the inscription

This marks the site
of Samuel Horn's Fort
1777

The stone is about three feet high, faces the railroad and the river, is mounted on a concrete platform about six feet square and is enclosed by an iron rail fence about ten feet square. A small American flag waves gently in the breezes in front of the stone. The view from the site of the Fort is picturesque and fascinating. Facing the river one sees fertile plains and rolling hills in the foreground; on the left, wooded hills. Turning to the right one can see for a distance of at least a dozen miles the Bald Eagle Mountain standing out majestically—the Roundtop, Kearns Mountain, Augenbaugh Mountain, and their nearby sister mountains in the Bald Eagle chain. The dreamy and winding Susquehanna, flowing through a beautiful valley, cuts directly under the sheer and commanding bluff on which Horn's Fort stood.

The Indians of Pennsylvania in general were friendly to the early white settlers. William Penn sought their good will and instead of seizing the land that belonged to them he bought the land from them. Tract after tract was purchased by William Penn and his sons who succeeded him as proprietors of Pennsylvania.

William Penn had treated the Indians justly but after his death his sons, who were anxious to acculate more wealth, virtually robbed the Indians of much of their land, as for instance, by the "Walking Purchase" in September 1737. White settlers moved towards the Alleghenies and gradually the Indians came to realize that they were being cheated out of their birthright.

Because of the unjust treatment that the Indians received they joined the French in the French and Indian War in 1755 and the British in the Revolutionary War in the late 1770's and wreaked vengeance on the white settlers on the Pennsylvania frontier by scalping them and burning their homes. The ravages of the Indians in Pennsylvania continued for forty years, from 1755 to 1795; from the time of the massacre at Penn's Creek to the Treaty of Greenville. During those forty years Pennsylvanians erected forts in almost all parts of the frontier to protect white families from the Indians.

THE MARKER AT SITE OF HORN'S FORT

In the middle of the 1700's the West Branch Valley and the surrounding territory which embraced a large part of North Central Pennsylvania was the reserved hunting and fishing ground of the Iroquois, the Delaware-Monsey and the Shawnee Indians. Adventurous white settlers pushed farther and farther into this domain. The redmen yielded reluctantly. In 1768 the Treaty of Fort Stanwix was signed. It gave the white men claim to a large belt of land running from the northeastern part of the state to the southwestern corner of Pennsylvania.

The treaty reserved all the land in Northwestern Pennsylvania to the Indians. A line drawn from Towanda to Pittsburgh through Williamsport and Clearfield would pretty closely follow the line drawn by the Treaty of Fort Stanwix which marked off the dividing line between red and white soil. According to this treaty the Susquehanna River was the boundary between red territory and white in the section now lying within Clinton County. Consequently, in 1768 the southern bank of the Susquehanna in present Clinton County was open to the pioneers but the northern shore was recognized as Indian property, "forbidden land" as far as the white man was concerned.

The first white settlers who came to what is now Clinton County arrived in 1768. They did not honor the treaty of Fort Stanwix. Quite a few of these settlers crossed the river and built their cabins on Indian soil. Practices of this sort did not improve the feelings of the Indian towards the white man. During the Revolution the British bribed the Indians to plunder and murder the settlers on the frontier. The Indians became more hostile and descended upon the settlers of the West Branch with a fury. A line of forts was built from Sunbury to Lock Haven. The forts which protected the settlers in the Clinton County area were Fort Antes, opposite the present site of Jersey Shore, Horn's Fort, between Pine Station and McElhattan, and Reid's Fort, at Lock Haven.

Fort Antes was built by Lieutenant Colonel Henry Antes in 1778, Horn's Fort was built by Samuel Horn in 1777, and Reid's Fort was built in 1777, probably by William Reid. Fort Augusta, at Sunbury, was the base of military operations for the North and West Branch valleys. The line of forts was garrisoned by soldiers at times but the matter of defense against Indian attacks fell chiefly upon the settlers in the neighborhood of the respective forts and the most capable of these men had already left to join the Revolutionary Army. When there was danger of an attack by the Indians the settlers would hurry to the nearest fort.

The Indian menace increased and early in June, 1778, Colonel Hunter, of Fort Augusta, sent a message up the West Branch Valley warning all the settlers to flee for their lives, as the Indians were planning a heavy attack to wipe out the settlers. Communities were panic stricken. Cabins, clearings and forts were deserted and people floated down the Susquehanna in canoes, boats, rafts and even in hog troughs, carrying their belongings with them. It was an exodus by a fear-stricken people. All the white settlers west of the Muncy Hills fled down the river. This flight is known in Pennsylvania history as the "Great Runaway" and it is an event that probably has no parallel in Pennsylvania frontier history. The settlers did not return to the upper end of the valley until 1783, five years after their dash for safety.

TYPICAL SCENE IN CENTRAL PENNSYLVANIA IN THE MID 1770's
Settlers lived in log houses, raised crops in their clearings, depended on horses and small boats for transportation, and crowded into a neighboring stockade for protection when the Indians were on the warpath.

The first settlers who came to the section that we now call Clinton County found a dense forest. They had to clear land in order to find a place to build a cabin and plant corn. It was an easy matter for a lone wily Indian to lie in wait in the thick woods and pounce on a white man. Most of these settlers were Scotch-Irish, and possessed the heartiness and bravery that was characteristic of the Scotch-Irish of those days. Because of their common danger they stuck close together.

Samuel Horn settled in the vicinity of Pine Station and built a log house on a high flat that extends out into a bend of the river. From his house he could get a good view up and down the valley. His cabin had a commanding position. The site of his log house along the Pennsylvania Railroad track is a few hundred yards east of the New York Central Railroad river bridge. In 1777 when the Indians excited fear, Horn, with the aid of his neighbors, built a stockade around his cabin. The stockade may have enclosed a quarter of an acre and became the fortress of the community in times of danger and was resorted to by settlers on the south bank and the "squatters" on the forbidden north bank.

Continental troops were scanty and few soldiers could be apportioned to the various forts. Most of the forts on the West Branch were defensive and were held by the settlers. It is said that a few soldiers were stationed at Horn's Fort. The pioneers on both sides of the river aided these soldiers in scouting and in spreading alarms to unsuspecting settlers. Several times the men of Horn's Fort had clashes with the Indians which resulted in the loss of a few lives. Small groups of Indians hovered around the fort in the hope of getting a few scalps. It was not safe for a white person to saunter around a quarter of a mile away from the stockade. One day in 1778 a young woman by the name of Ann Carson went beyond the stockade and was shot at by a hidden Indian. The bullet went through the folds of her dress, piercing fourteen holes in it, but she escaped unharmed. Another young woman by the name of Jane Anesley, at about the same time, was shot at several times by an Indian while she was milking a cow one evening just outside the stockade. One bullet cut through her dress and just grazed her body. Tradition has it that Horn's Fort was a defensive post and a valuable haven of refuge for the early settlers.

The Indians were causing a great deal of trouble in 1777 and early in 1778. Then, in June 1778, there came a fearful message to all the settlers in the West Branch Valley. Colonel Hunter sent his message up the valley. All white people were warned to flee down the river if they valued their lives. The great scout, Robert Copenhoven, carried the message from Fort Muncy to Fort Antes. Another messenger brought the news from Fort Antes to Horn's Fort. All the settlers for several miles around, from the north side and the south side of the river, assembled at Horn's Fort. This panicky group probably numbered more than one hundred in all. Plans were made at once to flee for safety. Cabins and crops were deserted and personal possessions that could not easily be carried down the river were buried. Soon after Colonel Hunter's message arrived, a party of four men left Horn's Fort in canoes, bound for Antes Fort to get a flat on which to carry their families down the river. Three of these four men were scalped by Indians at Pine Creek riffles on the return trip to Horn's Fort. The fourth man escaped narrowly by swimming in the lee of his canoe to the north bank of the river. On this same day settlers who were driving cattle "down river" were attacked by Indians a short distance from Horn's Fort. The settlers returned fire and wounded one Indian. The plundering band of Indians retreated at once. One white man had been hit and he was carried to Horn's Fort. These attacks increased the fears and anxiety of the men, women and children huddled within the stockade at Horn's Fort. They left for Sunbury as quickly as possible and arrived safely at Fort Augusta along with other refugees from Fort Muncy, Fort Antes and Reid's Fort, an army of several hundred people all told. The women and children and the possessions floated down the river on anything that would carry them, while the men walked in single file on each bank of the river in order to guard the women and children.

Little is known of Samuel Horn and no traces of his fort remain today. Records indicate that he was one of the two supervisors of Bald Eagle Township (then including the site of Horn's Fort which is now in Wayne Township) in 1774, and one of the two overseers of Bald Eagle Township in 1775. The assessment list of Bald Eagle Township made on January 4, 1786, includes his name and indicates that he was married. He evidently returned to Clinton County after the "Great Runaway." The last traces of the pioneer outpost named for him were destroyed in the years 1856-58 when the Philadelphia and Erie Railroad (now the Pennsylvania Railroad) was extended through Clinton County. The roadbed was cut through the northern end of the ground enclosed by the stockade and clear evidence of the stockade was found at that time.

Note. The information contained in this article was obtained mainly from two works; (1) Vol. 1, *Frontier Forts of Pennsylvania,* second edition, 1916, and (2) John Blair Linn's *History of Centre and Clinton Counties.* In 1893 the Pennsylvania legislature authorized the appointment of a commission to make a study of the frontier forts of Pennsylvania built prior to 1783. The commission printed its report in book form in 1896. The large volume on the history of Centre and Clinton Counties by John Blair Linn, of Bellefonte, was published in 1883.

XVIII

Applebutter-Making Time

The early settlers in Clinton County produced nearly everything they used. They built their own houses and barns, raised their crops, livestock, poultry and vegetables, baked their own bread, made "spreads," canned and dried food for the winter, "butchered" and smoked meat, raised flax and sheep, spun their own linen and wool and made their own clothing. They also made their own soap and brooms and burned the lime that they used to fertilize their farms. They were almost completely independent of the outside world.

The early Clinton Countians worked together. In the earliest days when one person wished to clear land or erect a building, a logging bee or a barn or house raising was held and the work was quickly done. Serenadings were vigorously entered into and much time was spent preparing the "horse fiddles" and other noisy devices for these occasions. "Apple schnitzings," corn husking and firewood cutting in the fall, butcherings in early December, "quiltin's" in the winter and "flittin's" on April 1st were often community affairs. At these gatherings everyone pitched in and worked and then enjoyed good food, games, singing, and storytelling.°

Many of these fine old customs disappeared as the towns grew in size and as the automobile took the place of the "spring wagon" and "buggy." But this time of the year [October] is applebutter-making time and as we go through the valleys and mountains during the next week or two and see people working industriously around the large kettles and woodpiles at "kettle place" on the farm, we can again picture the customs of thirty or forty years ago. Applebutter is still made by many of the farmers in Clinton County, and in much the same way as it was made more than a generation ago.

Applebutter is made by boiling and seasoning cider and apples. It is done on a large scale, being boiled in a big kettle over an open fire. It is made in batches of from eight to fourteen gallons at a batch. A big day's work is required to make a single batch or kettle of applebutter.

° Butchering was even more important than applebutter-making. Butchering adjacent to the house was a common occurrence, especially near Thanksgiving after the pigs born in spring had become large. Calves, and cows no longer of much use for producing calves or milk, were butchered in any part of the year cold enough to cool the carcasses after they had been scalded and hung on a tripod, and when flies and gnats would not be a nuisance.

Most farms had a "kettle place" where the applebutter was made and where the butchering and soap-making were done. Two upright posts supported a horizontal pole so that kettles could be hung on the pole directly over bonfires built between the upright posts.

The applebutter kettle was made of copper and sometimes of brass, rather than of iron, due to the "eating" acid properties of iron. The large iron "butchering kettles" were not used for applebutter-making due to the fact that the chemical reaction of cider on iron would poison a batch of applebutter. The kettles varied in size from about twenty gallons capacity to at least fifty-two gallons capacity, were from two and a half to three feet in

BUTCHERING, LIKE APPLEBUTTER-MAKING, WAS LARGELY AN OUTDOOR OPERATION, NEAR THE KITCHEN

This group of men and women paused to be photographed during their butchering operation at Youngdale, Wayne Township, Clinton County, at the north foot of the Bald Eagle Mountain, about 1932. Carcasses of two hogs are on the tripods.

Butchering began early in the morning, sometimes before daybreak, with the building of an outdoor fire under an enormous cast iron kettle. When the water began to boil a hog was killed and one end of the carcass was dipped into a barrel that had been filled with boiling water. After both ends were dipped the carcass was suspended from a tripod. The bristles, now loosened by the scalding, were scraped off. While hanging from the tripod the carcass was opened and the entrails were removed. The carcass was cut into large pieces. On the butchering bench it was cut into hams, shoulders, bacon, ribs, backbone, and sirloin. "Pudding," "ponhoss," and lard were cooked in the large kettle over the open fire. The sausage was ground outdoors or in the kitchen but was stuffed in the kitchen, into intestines that had been cleaned laboriously. Butchering three hogs was a big day's work for several men and women operating in an assembly-line fashion.

diameter and from two to two and a half feet in depth. They had a large handle like that of an ordinary bucket and were a bit wider at the top rim than at the bottom and had no legs. Applebutter kettles were shaped almost like an ordinary boiler that we use to cook potatoes in for supper, except that they had a rounded rather than a flat bottom. Applebutter kettles were expensive and delicate, but with care lasted for years. Some of these kettles still in use today are eighty or ninety years old. When they were new they sold for thirty, forty and even as high as sixty dollars each, and at country sales second hand kettles in good condition frequently brought almost as high a price as a new one. The brass kettles, which were scarce, sold for a still higher price than the copper ones. Applebutter kettles were adapted to practically nothing but applebutter making and were used only five or six days each year by most families. Because of the great cost and the few days of use each year, there were only a few applebutter kettles in each community and these were loaned from one family to another.

Applebutter-making required a great deal of skill. The cider had to be used before it became too hard. The proper proportion of cider and "schnitz" (peeled and sliced apples) had to be used. The amount of boiling necessary before the "schnitz" were put in and of boiling before removing the kettle from the fire were weighty decisions to be made. Flavoring in itself was a bit of an art. Firing also required experience, for there was great danger of scorching the kettle and burning the batch of applebutter if it was not kept boiling continuously or if it boiled too high when it was almost ready to be taken off the fire. On very windy or very rainy days firing was a difficult job. The wind blew the heat of the fire away from the kettle, or the rain drenched the fire and the attendants, unless a temporary windbreak or roof was thrown up at the kettle place.

Applebutter-making was a great event in the routine of almost every family. The job was a big one. When applebutter-making season arrived in the latter part of September and the early part of October, a date was set for the "boiling" several days in advance, so that arrangements could be made for borrowing the kettle and laying aside the regular household and farm duties. Scrubby and "down" apples were picked and ground into cider a day or two before the boiling was to begin. Choice apples for "schnitzing" were picked on the day they were to be schnitzed or a day before. A large pile of dry chestnut wood was carried to the kettle place at least a day before the boiling was to be done. If for some reason the applebutter "boiling" could not be carried through within two or three days after the cider was made, the cider was put away for vinegar or boiled until it was syrupy so that it would keep for several weeks for applebutter-making.

The job of making a batch of applebutter usually began after supper one day and ended sometimes as late as midnight of the next day. The schnitzing was done and the kettle borrowed in the evening and the boiling was begun in the morning. Approximately sixty-five gallons of cider and two bushels of schnitz were boiled in one batch, which yielded about fourteen gallons of applebutter. The biggest task connected with applebutter-making is the apple schnitzing, as any one who has helped to make applebutter knows.

When the schnitzing was to be done, five or six families would visit the family that was ready for applebutter-making. Everybody joined in the schnitzing operation enthusiastically and frequently the job was finished in two hours' time. Many interesting stories of spooks, witches, lumbering and hunting were told while the men, women and children were schnitzing apples, and all joined in singing the favorite old songs. Cider and apples were passed around as refreshments and when the work was finished many games were played. After several hours of merriment the visiting families went to their homes and the host family hurried to bed to catch a few hours' sleep.°

The family making the applebutter was on the job several hours before daylight. The wife or one of the girls washed the kettle while the husband or one of the sons built the fire. The copper kettles corroded slightly in a few hours' time and took on a greenish look. The women washed the insides of these kettles with salt and vinegar on the morning of the boiling. The salt and vinegar brightened the kettle until it shone. It was rinsed with water and hung on the hook dangling from the horizontal pole of the kettle place. The kettle was filled with cider. The fire was lighted and the cider was boiling before daybreak.

A brisk fire was kept and the cider was boiled down and down until it became a syrup. As the cider in the kettle boiled down, more cider was added and the kettle was kept as full as possible without running the risk of having it boil over. Sometimes two small applebutter kettles were used at the same time by one family when a large one could not be secured. The boiling down process was continued until the sixty-five gallons of cider and two bushels of schnitz could all be put in one kettle. Sixty-five gallons of cider were boiled down to about sixteen gallons, or four to one.

°Mrs. Roy G. Rich remembers as many as five families gathering on top of the Bald Eagle Mountain for an apple schnitzing party during the period 1918-1932. Of course applebutter had been made over an outdoor fire on valley farms and also in Southeastern Pennsylvania in the late nineteenth and early twentieth centuries. It is doubtful, however, that apple schnitzing parties were common in Pennsylvania after 1918 except in farm communities far back in the mountains.

AN APPLE SCHNITZING PARTY

This picture is reproduced from H. L. Fischer's book in the Pennsylvania German dialect, **'S Alt Marik-Haus Mittes In D'r Schtadt, un Die Alte' Zeite'** *(The Old Market House in the Middle of the City and The Olden Time), 1879, page 101. This picture seems to show that applebutter was made* **during** *the schnitzing party. The folks on the Bald eagle Mountain did not begin to boil the cider until making an outdoor fire early the next morning. They added the apple slices after the cider had boiled for several hours over an outdoor fire.*

The schnitz were added to the cider almost any time between ten o'clock and noon, depending on how early in the morning the cider began to boil, and also upon how high and even the fire under it was kept. A bucketful of schnitz was poured into the kettle at a time and two or three hours elapsed from the time the first bucketful was added until the last schnitz were thrown in.

There is a danger of scorching a batch of applebutter if apple schnitz sink to the bottom of the kettle. To avoid scorching, the cider and schnitz were stirred almost constantly, from a few minutes after the time the first schnitz were put into the kettle until the applebutter was made.

The task was a wearisome one and continued from about noontime to, frequently, as late as midnight. So as to be able to stir without getting close to the flames of the fire a wooden handle about eight to ten feet long was attached at right angles to a wooden paddle about five inches wide and about three feet long.

The stirrer looked like the letter "L" with the handle forming the stem and the paddle the base of the letter. About half a dozen holes, approximately an inch in diameter, were bored in the paddle of the stirrer. Two of these holes were bored within about an inch of the bottom of the paddle for the purpose of attaching two corn husk brushes. Green corn husks were plucked and washed and pushed through these two bottom holes of the stirrer paddle. The free ends of the corn husks were pulled together, tied with a string, and trimmed in such a way as to make them look like two small separate brushes or tassels on the end of the paddle.

STIRRING THE CIDER AND THE APPLE SLICES

This picture shows a two-kettle operation. The wooden paddle used for stirring had a long handle so that the person doing the stirring could escape the heat and smoke of the fire. The cooking and stirring continued throughout much of the day and late into the night.

The corn husks were used for two reasons. They protected the thin and delicate copper bottom of the kettle from being scratched or bumped hard by the wooden paddle and they made stirring more effective. As a brush is more adapted than a stick to scrubbing the bottom of a pan, just so the corn husk brushes were more effective in keeping syrupy schnitz from sticking to the bottom of the kettle than the bare wooden paddle would have been.

The purpose of the other holes in the stirrer paddle were to "fine" the schnitz. As the broad paddle was moved back and forth, a current of cider passed through the holes and around the edge of it. As the schnitz cooked soft they broke and flowed in the current of the cider through the holes. As the soft schnitz flowed through the holes they were washed and worn finer and finer until at last they were cooked and stirred into mush.

In spite of the constant stirring, frequently batches of applebutter were scorched before anyone was aware of the fact. If the bottom of the kettle felt rough to the person stirring, or if black specks rose to the top of the cider and schnitz, one knew at once that the batch was burning on the bottom of the kettle. If the kettle was not removed at once there was danger that the entire batch would be so badly burned that it would not be palatable.

As soon as there was a well-founded suspicion that the batch was scorching, the kettle was taken off the fire and the contents dipped into containers. The tedious job of scouring the bottom of the kettle was begun at once. Care had to be taken to avoid piercing a hole in the thin bottom of the copper kettle. Cleaning a burned kettle was a slow and dreaded task. When the kettle was burned badly, small chunks of the burned schnitz would float around in the partly cooked applebutter. As many of these black chunks as possible were fished out of the hot mixture in the temporary containers with a spoon.

As soon as the kettle was cleaned and the burnt chunks were fished out, the unfinished applebutter was put back into the kettle, hung in place over the fire, and boiled again. If scorching was detected in time it was not a serious matter, only an inconvenient one. But if the kettle was badly burned, the job of cleaning the kettle became very difficult and the applebutter took on a decidedly burnt and unpleasant taste.

From the time the kettle was hung in place over the fire before dawn until the schnitz were added, about noontime, the only task to be done was firing and adding cider. But all during the afternoon and evening the task was a two-fold one, that of firing and stirring. The batch of cider and schnitz in the kettle was boiled until it was thick and black. It was stirred until the person in the family who knew most about the art of making applebutter pronounced that it was ready "to come off," which was usually late at night. Then two people lifted the kettle off the hook by means of a pole thrust through the handle or by grasping the hot handle with cloths in their hands. The kettle was set down very carefully, as the weight of the applebutter could easily dent the thin bottom of the copper kettle if it would be set down roughly. Something soft, such as a burlap bag, was laid on the ground and the kettle was placed on it so as to avoid the danger of small stones and grit wearing tiny holes in the bottom of the loaded kettle. A few copper kettles had double bottoms. An extra sheet of copper covering the bottom and extending a few inches up the sides was fastened on by a row of rivets extending around the top edge of this extra sheet. These double bottom kettles were rare and were more expensive than the ordinary kettles.

The applebutter continued to boil for a few minutes after it was taken off the fire and it was stirred for a short time after the kettle was placed on the bag on the ground, so as to avoid all danger of burning. It was then dipped out into white pine or red oak homemade kegs which had a capacity of from five to twenty gallons each. Red oak and white pine were the only kinds of wood used in making applebutter kegs. Red oak and white pine were used because they did not give the applebutter a woody taste. Most of the applebutter kegs were made of the soft white pine because it was the easier of the two to "work up" into kegs. A wooden lid shaped somewhat like the lid on an ordinary stewing kettle was made and put on top of the keg. The kegs filled with applebutter were carried to the kitchen at once and the family scurried off to bed, thankful that the big task was over. The applebutter was cool by the next morning and the kegs were carried to the garret or the "spare room," or any out of the way place in the house where there was no danger that the applebutter would mold. Applebutter was dipped out of the kegs as it was needed.

The farmers of Clinton County made several batches of applebutter every year. A farmer made about twelve to fourteen gallons to the batch and might have seven or eight "boilings" in a month's time. There was a great sale for applebutter then and many a family made as high as one hundred gallons of this "spread" each fall for their own use and for "market." Sugar was not used in making applebutter but the farmers had three different seasonings. They used sassafras, cinnamon and cloves. They usually seasoned at least one batch with sassafras, one with cinnamon and one with cloves.

Dried or fresh peelings of the outer layer of the root of the sassafras tree were used in giving applebutter a sassafras flavor. About a handful of these peelings were put in a small cloth sack. This sack was tied shut with a string and dropped into the kettle about an hour before it was ready to be taken off of the fire. The ground cinnamon or ground cloves was sprinkled in, a teaspoonful to the gallon.

When farmers had a plentiful crop of pears and peaches they made pear butter and peach butter by boiling pear schnitz in cider and peach schnitz in cider at the kettle place. Occasionally a kettle of pumpkin butter was made by boiling pumpkin schnitz in cider over the open fire.

The applebutter that was made forty years ago was very black and very strong or bitter. It contained no sugar and was boiled down very much. Today a twelve or fourteen gallon batch of applebutter is made from about twenty-five gallons of cider and one and a half bushels of schnitz as compared with twelve or fourteen gallon batches that were made from sixty-five gallons of cider and two bushels of schnitz a generation or more ago. Today cider is boiled down about "two to one" as compared with more than "four to one" previously. Sugar is used today and the applebutter now is soft, sweet and light in color. The "old time" black and bitter applebutter was so thick that it could be cut with a knife.

Today about a pound of sugar is used for every gallon of cider used. The sugar is added about an hour before the kettle is taken off the fire. There is a danger of the sugar sinking to the bottom and burning. To prevent this the sugar is dissolved in a few quarts of hot or cold boiled or unboiled cider and is poured into the kettle slowly while someone stirs the cider and schnitz in the kettle with the large stirrer.

The same three flavors, sassafras, cinnamon and cloves are used today and the applebutter is still seasoned in the same way with the exception that it is not "boiled" as long and sugar is used. Today the cider is not boiled nearly as long as formerly nor are the schnitz boiled as long as formerly.

The method of making applebutter forty years ago is commonly referred to as the "old way" and the shorter method of today is usually called the "new way." The same type of kettle is used. The old fashioned kettle places are still to be seen but some farmers use the "kettle ring" or "spider," an iron ring with three legs, on which the kettle is placed, rather than being suspended from a hook on a horizontal pole.

On many of the valley farms the kettle place is protected from the weather by a permanent roof. The same kind of stirrers with the corn husk brushes are used to this day. Many of the kettles and stirrers that are used today were used fifty and more years ago. Fires are kept high and as long as the cider and schnitz are boiling high many people will not stir, except when adding sugar, claiming that the boiling motion will prevent the schnitz from sinking to the bottom and causing the kettle to scorch.

Today less applebutter is made in Clinton County than was made several dozen years ago. The "new way" of making applebutter requires less cider, fewer schnitz, less boiling and little stirring. The kettle is started at daybreak or later rather than at three or four o'clock in the morning and is taken off at three or four o'clock in the afternoon rather than at ten or eleven o'clock or midnight. Instead of boiling the cider down and down it is boiled only until all the "scum" coming to the surface of the kettle can be scooped off and thrown away. Instead of boiling the cider and schnitz until the applebutter is thick and black they are boiled only until they "push a scum and draw no cider."

At various intervals during the afternoon a spoonful of applebutter is taken from the kettle and put on a saucer. When it cools someone pushes the applebutter from one side of the saucer to the other with the back of a spoon. If the applebutter has the consistency of mush and is watery when it is pushed with the spoon the batch is boiled longer. If the applebutter puckers up as though it had a skin on it, when it is pushed with the spoon, and if no cider gathers around the edges of the applebutter on the saucer it is considered to be ready "to come off."

Today the applebutter is poured into earthenware crocks, varying in size from one to six gallons capacity, rather than into homemade wooden kegs. The applebutter is brought in and put on the kitchen table as formerly and the next morning the tops of the crocks are covered with paper which is tied on with string. The applebutter is still stored in the garret or the spare room. Pear butter and peach butter are made when the pear and peach crops of the county are plentiful but it is doubtful if pumpkin butter is made to any noticeable extent in this section anymore, if at all.

Applebutter is still made in Clinton County in much the same way as it was made forty years ago except that now less of it is made, sugar is used and each batch is boiled less than formerly. The "new way" has displaced the "old way" and the apple schnitzing parties have almost completely disappeared. Even so, to this day, applebutter making is a great event among most farm families and the high priced copper kettles are still borrowed.

XIX

An Old-Time Fiddler

Fifty years ago barn dances and singing parties were popular forms of amusement in Clinton County. In those days each small community had to devise its own form of entertainment. People who could play and sing became popular. There was much playing and singing in the farm houses and in the lumber camps and frequently a group of people would assemble at a neighbor's house and play games and sing the old familiar songs in unison. In the sections where religious influence did not place a ban on dancing many barn dances were held. Dances were held in barns because there were no community halls large enough to accommodate a group of dancers. New barns were frequently "dedicated" by holding a dance in them. Barn dances were held on the "thrash floor" at husking bees, after the corn was husked. Hay rides in summertime and sleighing parties in winter often finished with a barn dance.

The music at a barn dance was usually furnished by a local "fiddler." Any one who could play a violin was in demand. The music was of fast tempo and loud. The dances were hilarious affairs and the swing of the dancers was much like that of the square dance of today. Fiddlers were eagerly sought and frequently were called from town to town to play at a frolic. The barn dance fiddler of a generation or so ago was not a polished musician but he was an entertainer and a unique character.

Barn dances are almost a thing of the past in the Pennsylvania mountains but a few of the old fiddlers still remain. One day I chanced upon a queer old barn dance fiddler when I was in quest of a muzzleloader gun. A bewhiskered woodsman had directed me to a certain Mr. Charles Bowman, of North Bend, a small town on the Susquehanna River near Renovo, and told me that Mr. Bowman had the gun, powder horn, bullet pouch and entire outfit that I was looking for. I was delighted and started out early for North Bend one morning without having the slightest idea what sort of a person Mr. Bowman was. I supposed that he was an ordinary person living at the edge of the town, and, perhaps, an elderly person who had worked in the woods in his earlier days.

After inquiring in North Bend as to Mr. Bowman's residence I was finally directed to a grassy trail that led into the mountains from the state highway at a point on the paved road about a mile from the edge of the little town. I trudged up the trail which was an old road grown over with high grass and brush. At each turn of the road I looked eagerly for a clearing and any kind of a dwelling. After traveling about a mile on this al-

THE OLD-TIME FIDDLER—MR. CHARLES BOWMAN

most abandoned, winding, hilly road I came in sight of an old log house perched on high ground in a small clearing at the head of a hollow. The old house was almost completely hidden by woods on all sides and by hills on three sides. It looked deserted, forlorn and aged. There was not a sign of human habitation; no one in the little yard, no faces at the windows, not even a wisp of smoke curling lazily from the chimney.

I approached the clearing and knocked on the kitchen door of the house. Silence. "Does any one live in this solitary spot?" "If so what kind of people are they?" "Is anyone at home?" Such were the questions that ran through my mind as I waited for a response to my rapping. Then—a sound? Yes, a footstep. I heard a man descending the stairway. In a few moments the kitchen door was unlocked noisily and an old man faced me. He was tall, straight, and thin, had white hair and a long white mustache. He was dressed in a blue chambray work shirt and blue overalls and was barefooted. I introduced myself and found that he was the man I was hunting, Mr. Charles Bowman. He invited me to come in and courteously ushered me to a comfortable chair in the kitchen.

As we began to chat I looked about, hither and yon. I had observed that the house was made of logs, was two stories high, was topped with a gable roof and that it had a cellar and a porch. Now I noticed that the logs were chinked with mud and that the interior was unplastered. The first floor was divided into two rooms, a "parlor" and a kitchen. The kitchen was a cozy little room but rather dark. A small writing desk and a table on one side, an old fashioned corner cupboard in one corner opposite the stairway, in another corner, an old dough-tray with legs, a couch, cook stove and a woodbox on the other side, a rifle hanging on the wall near the door and a few chairs in the center of the room comprised almost all the furnishings of the kitchen most of which were probably as old as the log house itself.

Mr. Bowman proved to be an interesting character and he entertained me royally. Bit by bit he told me the story of his life. I soon learned that he was very fond of music and that he was an old-time fiddler, that he was a bachelor and that he had lived in this log house nearly all his life. I also found that he was unable to read or write and that he did not even know his own age, and that he was his own physician, curing all his ills with herbs.

He proudly brought his favorite fiddle from the "parlor" and began to play for me. The strains of the song were beautiful and enchanting. They seemed to have the power to grip one and carry one away to a world of dreams. Even the fiddler himself seemed to be in a trance as he played. He was completely absorbed in his music. It seemed as though he had forgotten me. Then he finished the number and relaxed. Enthusiastically I asked him the name of the piece that he had just finished playing. I had not recognized it. He told me that he had never known the name of the piece but that one time a person had told him that it was a piece that Ole Bull, the world famous violinist who built his castle and his colony on Kettle Creek, Potter County, in 1853, used to play. The piece was so sweet and charming that I asked Mr. Bowman to play it again. He played it again and seemed pleased to do so.

He then played a number of familiar old barn dance pieces, marking time first with one bare foot and then with the other. He swung tune after tune out of his instrument in a light and airy fashion and I soon found myself marking time with my feet. He played the old popular pieces such as "Golden Slippers," "She'll Be Coming Round the Mountain," and "Turkey in the Straw." He showed me a second violin. He also produced a guitar and a mandolin and played each of them and sang a few songs.

Mr. Bowman was very proud of his instruments, especially the violins. He handled them as a mother would handle her infant child. Instead of using a block of rosin on his bow, as many violinists do, he scraped the block with his pocket knife and rubbed the powdered rosin on his bow. The first violin that he played for me he prized above his other instruments and ranked the second violin next. He invited me to examin his favorite instrument closely. It was a beautiful violin and had a fine tone. Dainty red and white ribbons were tied around its scroll. Deep holes, probably indicating great age and much use, were worn in the fingerboard. Mr. Bowman said that he had been told that this instrument might have been one of Ole Bull's at one time. He took me out on the porch in the sunlight and had me peer down through sound holes of the violin. On the inside of the instrument I saw the name Stradivarius and the date 1713.

The story of Mr. Bowman's life as he told it to me while we were seated comfortably in the cozy little old kitchen was intensely interesting. His grandfather had been a mule-team driver for an iron company, probably in Bald Eagle Valley, and had also been a charcoal burner. His father had worked on the Pennsylvania Canal in Clinton County, had helped to lay the pipe line for the oil company and had been a charcoal burner and a barn dance fiddler.

When Mr. Charles Bowman was a very small boy his father went away many evenings to play his fiddle at dances. Young "Charlie" would sit and listen to his dad play the violin at home and one day he asked him, "Pap, what makes the noise come out of that box?" His father answered him by saying that there was a little "nigger" in the fiddle and that every time he pulled his bow back and forth he was squeezing the little "nigger" and making him squeal and holler. Young "Charlie" was anxious to see that little "nigger" in the music box and he waited for his opportunity. One night his father went away without taking the fiddle with him. Charlie brought in wood and water and helped tidy up the kitchen for his mother, hoping to get her off to bed as quickly as possible. After she went to bed he seized the fiddle and his father's jack knife and hid in the stairway. He was determined to find the creature who made the noise for his father. He cut a large hole in the back of the violin but to his sheer disappointment he found nothing inside except the sound post, which is a small round stick of wood that touches the back and the face of the violin and brings out a rich mellow tone.

A short time after making this experiment his father gave Charlie lessons on the violin and he practiced industriously when his father went away at night to play for dances. Charlie wanted to become a master of the fiddle and he desired to become as good or better than his father at playing the violin. Frequently he would ask his mother "Can't I play as good as Pap?" She would answer, "Yes, as good, or better."

When Mr. Bowman was big enough to handle a pick and push a wheelbarrow he worked on the canal with his father, dredging, and filling leaks and washouts in the dikes. In 1881 he worked with his father for the pipe line company helping to lay the line. For many years Mr. Bowman and his father burned charcoal and sold it in Lock Haven and Williamsport. Laboring did not put an end to Mr. Bowman's musical career. He stuck to his fiddle and bought a new one every time he had an opportunity to do so, always hoping to find the violin of his dreams. He played for many a dance and at times travelled long distances with his fiddle. He played in Centre and Lycoming Counties, and in Sugar Valley, Lock Haven, Lusk Run, Charlton and other places in Clinton County.

Mr. Bowman took great delight in picturing the "old days." Barn dances were numerous and fiddlers were sought. The fiddlers had a great deal of endurance, often working all day and playing all night, until two or three o'clock or dawn. Drawing the bow for such great lengths of time was a severe strain but the old fiddlers stuck to the task valiantly. No admission was charged to these community dances but the hat was passed and a collection was taken for the fiddler. Quite often fiddlers could make a comfortable living by playing at night and in many instances made more money playing at the dances than they could earn on a laboring job when they were working for "day's wages."

The old fiddler spoke of sleighing parties that were held years ago. A teamster would drive thru a community with his "bobs," gather up a crowd and drive on to the home of the host family where the dance was to be held. As the jolly sleighers approached the home of the host the teamster would announce their arrival by blowing a hunting horn. Many of these sleigh parties and dances were held, many families taking their turn as host. Quite often the people flocked to the Bowmans' to spend the night in music and dancing.

The story of the old house and Mr. Bowman's reminiscences of his father were entertaining. Mr. Bowman lived in the log house ever since it was built. It was erected by his father and neighbors in a "house raising" in two days' time when Mr. Bowman was a very small boy. Prior to the "house raising" the Bowmans had lived on another farm "over the hill," about three miles distant from the present Bowman house.

From boyhood on the old fiddler followed his father from one job to another, from the canal to the pipe line and on through to charcoal burning and fiddling, all the while living at home and working the small farm of twelve acres. He delighted in telling that his father used to light his pipe with flint and steel, striking his jack knife on a piece of flint and using burned rags for tinder. In speaking of the endurance of the old fiddlers he proudly told how his father played for dances several nights with a bullet in his hand. His father had accidentally shot himself with a .22 calibre revolver and for days the wound was not properly dressed but he went on playing just the same.

Mr. Bowman was never married and he lived with his parents until they died. After his father died he cared for his mother. Since she died several years ago he has been trying to fight off lonesomeness by burying himself in music. He has almost isolated himself from other people by living alone on his little out-of-the-way farm. He no longer goes about the countryside playing for parties and, out of respect for his mother, he no longer entertains dancers at his house as formerly. A tinge of sadness hangs over the old fiddler, the log house wears a melancholy frown and the twelve acres which constitute the "farm" are nearly all grown up in bushes. The old fiddler still lives in the house of his childhood, carries water from the spring on the side of the hill behind the house, treks to his garden on top of the hill far above the log dwelling and plays his favorite fiddles, but for him the spark of hope has almost vanished. For him the old days are gone. For ourselves he is a link connecting us with the past.

Author's Note: Mr. Bowman proved to be an interesting character. The gun he showed me was a very old smooth-bore rifle with a long barrel and a small graceful stock. It is still in working condition and shoots fine shot as well as the solid ball. Mr. Bowman, however, was much more interested in his violins than in anything else. He claimed that he had been offered a large sum for each of them but had refused to part with either.

The name "Stradivarius" and the date "1713" caught my eye when he showed me his favorite fiddle, for Stradivarius of Cremona, Italy, was the most famous violin maker of all time and today his violins sell for thousands of dollars. I could not read all of the printing inside of the instrument, but Mr. Bowman pushed a chicken feather carefully down through one of the sound holes and brushed the powdered rosin aside so that I could read all the printing on the label inside the violin. Then I read "Antonius Stradivarius Cremonenlis Faciebat Anno 1713." To my chagrin I learned later that the "Old Masters" placed their stamp on the end of the neck of every violin they built, that thousands of violins are patterned today like violins made by Stradivarius and other famous violin makers, and that these imitations are marked with a paper label pasted inside of the violin. Mr. Bowman's fiddle may be a cheap imitation, but perhaps the old fiddler enjoys his instrument as much as Ole Bull, who had many violins, would have enjoyed Stradivarius' best violin.

When I asked Mr. Bowman how old he was he told me that he had "kinder lost track" but said he thought he was in the "seventies or eighties" and asked, "Don't you think I look it?" I told him that I did not think he looked quite that old. In a few minutes he disappeared into his "parlor" and came back to the kitchen with an old Bible. He handed it to me and said that I might be able to find something in it concerning his age. I began to page through it and found a loose scrap of paper in it on which were scrawled a few lines, partly unintelligible, in a laborious handwriting. In poor grammar it stated briefly: "Rashel, Bowman Yons Born December 23, 1805. Dide August 7, 1889, age 83 years 7 months 15 day." I read the note aloud and at once Mr. Bowman exclaimed "that was my grandmother" and he urged me to look further in the Bible.

In the back of the book on the page for inserting a record of births I found a notation which gave the year of Mr. Bowman's birth according to which he was sixty-seven years of age. All through his conversation I had noticed that Mr. Bowman had no conception of approximate dates. Things occurred when he was "very small" or "before his father died" or "since his mother died." He couldn't tell whether he had been ten or fifteen years old when a certain event took place and he could not even tell whether his father had died five or fifteen years ago. In one instance only could he recall the date of a specific event, and that was the year of the laying of the pipe line, 1881, and he had that date correct.

It seems almost unbelievable that there are people in Clinton County who cannot read or write and it is still more surprising to meet people who do not even know their own ages. At three different times I have met people in the Clinton County mountains who were in a sane mind and did not know their ages, one man telling me that he had "kinder lost count" since "the book that his mother kept them sorta things in disappeared."

In this article I have changed the name of the old-time fiddler and the location of his home so as to protect his identity, but I have given the facts as I observed them and the account just as he gave it to me.

XX

Mr. Never Fear

MR. NEVER FEAR APPROACHES THE "HAUNTED" HOUSE

There is something fascinating and alluring about an old log house. A certain indescribable charm hovers over such a dwelling. The early settlers in North America built their homes in the New World with logs. The pioneers who pushed west from the Atlantic coast towards the Alleghenies and later towards the plains and the Rockies and then on to the Pacific coast lived in log houses (and adobe in some almost treeless Western areas) and called these structures "Home."

Princeton University, Washington and Jefferson College and Dickinson College grew out of the "Log College" which was built on the Neshaminy in Bucks County, Pennsylvania, sometime before 1725 by William Tennent, a Presbyterian minister. Three of Pennsylvania's famous log buildings that are still in existence and are being carefully preserved are of particular interest. The old Quaker Meeting House at Catawissa, near Bloomsburg, was built in the year 1785. Although services are no longer held in that building the old church is in an excellent state of preservation. The church lawn and the adjoining cemetery, which are near the center of the town, are kept as neat and as attractive as any private lawn.

The log house in which President James Buchanan was born on April 23, 1791, at Cove Gap (Foltz) in Franklin County, Pennsylvania, has been removed to Chambersburg. [In 1974 the log building is on the Campus of Mercersburg Academy, Mercersburg, Pennsylvania. However, there is serious question that the log building that is preserved at Mercersburg is the one in which Buchanan was born].

The original log academy of Dr. John McMillan, said to be the oldest existing school building west of the Allegheny Mountains, stands on the campus of Washington and Jefferson College today. This log building was erected in about the year 1780 and was the real beginning of Jefferson College at Canonsburg, which later was merged with Washington College to form the present Washington and Jefferson College at Washington, in Southwestern Pennsylvania.

Many log dwellings were built in Clinton County. A few of them still remain but most of them have vanished. Many people still living in the vicinity of Lock Haven like to talk of their younger days that were spent in these comfortable buildings.

As was typical of the frontier the first log dwellings in Clinton County were very crude affairs. The crude log cabin gradually developed into the neater and more serviceable log house. A second story was added. Walls and ceilings were plastered and cellars were dug. These homes were frequently built in two days' time at a "house raising." The log house became a very comfortable building in which to live. It was cool in the summertime and easily heated in wintertime. Many a fine old legend has been told in these old log houses. And many a fine old legend that lives to this day has its scene laid in one of these snug and picturesque old dwellings that are surrounded in our minds by alluring and captivating imaginations.

In the late 1890's or the early years of the 1900's one of the last log houses in the vicinity of Youngdale was destroyed by fire. It was a two-story building, had a cellar and a cook stove and a "room" stove. One winter evening about forty years ago the engineer and fireman on a New York Central train approaching Youngdale noticed that this old log house was on fire. The engineer stopped his train and the crew rushed in to extinguish the flames. They entered the burning building and found an old mother sleeping in a bed in a room on the first floor and found two of her grown sons sleeping soundly upstairs. The men and their mother were roused and pulled from the burning log house just before the roof caved in. They narrowly escaped being burned to death.

A short time ago one of the sons who was rescued from the burning log house at Youngdale told me a weird story about that very dwelling which probably was handed down for a hundred years. It is a story based on the supernatural but it is different from most witch stories. After becoming familiar with the story one might almost wonder whether some person had spun home a moral lesson. My friend, who is now almost sixty years old, has "followed the woods" all his life and grew up in an atmosphere saturated with superstitious beliefs. When he was a boy thirteen or fourteen years old his grandmother used to tell him the story of Mr. Never Fear. The story was supposed to have taken place in about 1850, when his grandmother was a girl just out of her teens; in the glorious days before the Civil War when large freight boats and swiftly moving packet boats carried freight and passengers up the West Branch Valley on the canal in summertime and when the stage coaches kept a line of communication open with the east in the wintertime. It was in the days before the large lumber camps opened in Central Pennsylvania, in the days when the settled portion of Clinton County was made up mainly of farmers.

The story was as follows: A Mr. Shadey was hotel keeper in the quaint little town that we know as McElhattan. Shadey was doing a prosperous business. He was born and raised in the log house already referred to, and lived there with his mother all during his boyhood. His mother lived at the "old homestead" until the end of her life. She had saved a tidy sum during her lifetime and this she hid before she died.

It was commonly known that old Mrs. Shadey had money but after she passed away no one knew where it was. Her son, the hotel keeper, became owner of her log house and its scant furnishings. The house was a comfortable one for that day and Shadey hoped that he might rent it and turn it into a source of income. A number of tenants moved into the house and out again. No tenant stayed very long, none more than three weeks. Each tenant came back to Shadey with the story that the house was "spooked," "haunted," or visited by "evil spirits," "ghosts" and "witches." Gradually people in the community began to believe the corresponding stories of the various tenants of the old log house, and the old Shadey homestead came to be known as "haunted."

The hotel keeper became exceedingly perplexed about the mysterious affair. He wanted to have the foulness of superstition removed from the home of his childhood and he wanted to solve the mystery that darkened his mother's doorstep. He offered the log house "rent free" to any person who would live in it. This inducement failed to attract a long-term tenant. Coming to his wit's end, Mr. Shadey publicly announced that he would give a clear deed for the old homestead to any one who would live in the log house.

Time dragged along, bringing no satisfactory results to the hotel keeper until one winter afternoon a young man approached Shadey, announcing that he would like to accept the hotel keeper's offer and move into the log house. Mr. Shadey had been approached by many "brave" men who had moved into the log house and soon moved out again. He lost faith in the "self confidence" of the "applicant" and when this latest applicant appeared before him in the hotel on a winter afternoon Shadey attempted to discourage him and intimated that he would not have enough grit to "stick it out" at the log house. The young man straightened, looked squarely at the hotel keeper and said "My name is Never Fear." Shadey must have been impressed for he gave the keys to the young man and sent him to the old homestead at Youngdale, a mile distant.

Mr. Never Fear packed in some provisions and went to the log house immediately, alone. The first evening was a cold one. The snow had fallen deeply the night before but the young adventurer managed to get in some wood and water and make himself comfortable before darkness fell upon him. He prepared his supper by lamplight and as he was about to cook his potatoes, meat and dried beans he heard a squeaking noise in back of him. He turned and noticed that the cellar door was opening slowly. Then out came a large black dog. It walked across the kitchen floor and disappeared as mysteriously as it had approached. Mr. Never Fear held his nerve. He was not seized with terror but he was puzzled. The next day was a beautiful one and he spent it by cutting wood and pondering on thoughts of the strange dog. The play of the sunshine on the snow-covered earth delighted him but nothing could drive the thoughts of the phantom dog from his mind.

On the second evening the new tenant again prepared his evening meal by lamplight. The wind was howling and a storm was brewing. The wind screeched through the forest and then died down until it soughed through the pines in a melancholy way, only to increase again in its velocity and terrorizing shrillness. After Mr. Never Fear had cooked his meal he sat down to eat it, alone. To eat a meal by lamplight in a lonely haunted house on a black, cold, stormy winter evening all by one's self is not an attractive prospect.

No sooner had Never Fear started to eat his meal than things began to happen. The cellar door opened slowly and creakily. A man emerged from the cellar-way. Then a coffin. And then another man. Two men carrying a coffin! They walked across the kitchen and seemed to pay no attention

"MY NAME IS NEVER FEAR, WHAT DO YOU HAVE IN THAT COFFIN?"

whatsoever to the young man who had started to eat his supper. The young tenant must have been plucky for he spoke up boldly, saying "My name is Never Fear, what do you have in that coffin?" The two men carrying the coffin stopped and the man at the head of the coffin said, "It was lucky for you that you spoke or you would have been in the coffin, too." Both men turned and carried their coffin back to the cellar door. The man at the head of the coffin beckoned to Never Fear and told him to follow them.

They went down the cellar steps and Never Fear picked up his oil lamp and followed them. Down the creaky stairs into the black cellar they went on that stormy winter night. The men with the coffin went to one corner of the cellar. The man at the head of the coffin pointed to a large rock lying on the cellar floor. He said to Never Fear, "Move that rock and you may have anything that you find under it."

Never Fear looked at the rock. It was of enormous size, probably weighing four hundred pounds. He shook his head and said that it was beyond his power to lift that rock. The man at the head of the coffin replied, "My body put it there. Your body can take it away." Never Fear looked at the rock again and then took off his coat, rolled up his sleeves and pulled and tugged until he could feel the stone moving ever so little. He worked and worked and finally succeeded in rolling the stone to one side. He was surprised to find a pitcher filled with gold coins under the rock. He looked up but found that the two men and their coffin had disappeared.

Never Fear took the pitcher of money and climbed the stairs to the kitchen. He hid the pitcher and the money carefully and waited for new developments. For several days he turned over in his mind the mysterious doings of the first two nights. Nothing new occurred. He was not disturbed again by strange visitors. He then decided that he would go to McElhattan and speak to the hotel keeper. He met Shadey, reminded him of his bargain, and asked for a deed to the log house. After slight hesitation Shadey procured the deed and the bargain was settled. Never Fear, now having the deed safely tucked in his pocket, urged Shadey to come to Youngdale to the log house, stating that he had something of interest to show the hotel keeper.

The two men started for the old log house and upon their arrival Never Fear told Shadey about the dog and the men with the coffin, and showed the hotel keeper the pitcher of gold coins. As soon as Shadey saw the pitcher of money he gasped and said, "That was my mother's pitcher. You can have the money but let me have the pitcher."

The moral of the story probably was this: Old Mrs. Shadey was a wise woman and wished to leave her wealth only to a worthy person. She hid her money before death and then re-appeared on earth in various forms, so as to test men's courage. The faint-hearted were scared away by her but the person with courage she guided to her treasure. Stories with a similar plot were told time and again in Clinton County in private homes and in the lumber camps.

XXI

The Purring Panthers

This folktale was told to Dr. George Swetnam, Feature Writer, *Pittsburgh Press.* It was told to him in the early 1950's by Mr. Hi Cranmer, then postmaster at the village of Hammersley Fork on Kettle Creek in Clinton County. Mr. Cranmer had heard the tale in about 1890 from old men. The tale was published in the *Pittsburgh Press* under date of July 22, 1962. In writing the article for the *Press,* Dr. Swetnam told the story in the backwoods language of about 1890, the vernacular used by Mr. Cranmer when sharing the account with Dr. Swetnam. This folktale is reproduced, here, with Dr. Swetnam's permission.

° ° ° °

Old man Jake Woodley, they say, was the first white man to settle in the northern part of Clinton County, away back around the year 1800.

He worked for a land company that had taken up thousands of acres, most of it in what's now the State Forest, and he built himself a cabin beside Kettle Creek—up on the Hammersley Fork.

Jake wasn't so old then, and he got along all right back there in the hills. He got there towards winter, with a yoke of oxen he could kill and eat if he ran out of food; and he built a good tight cabin with a stick-and-mud chimney, and a lean-to alongside for the stock.

But hunting was good that year, and Jake didn't have to kill his animals to get along. He'd brought along some flour, and he killed some deer and bears, and wild turkeys, and now and then a mess of squirrels for a change. Once he killed a panther, and he always said it tasted just like veal.

Before spring come around he'd cleared himself a little patch of land, and he deadened some trees by girdling 'em, and some more with fire, and scrubbed out the bushes and underbrush pretty good. He'd brought along some seed, and he planted himself some corn, and some tobacco, and some turnips. They didn't grow potatoes in these parts then, but he got some artichoke roots from an Indian, and some squash seed, and planted those.

MOUNTAIN MAN
JAKE WOODLEY

Low On Salt

Things growed pretty good in that new ground, but along about time for frost, Jake run out of salt, and that wasn't good. His powder and lead was gettin' low, too, an' he seen he had to do something right away.

So Jake went out in the woods an' cut a big white-oak tree, an' sawed off four rounds about the same size, for a set of wheels. He made holes in the center, and hardened 'em with fire, an' he hewed out a pair of axles, and put pins through the ends to keep the wheels from comin' off. Then he squared some timbers and nailed 'em to one axle, and he hooked that bed to the front axle with a big oak pin so's it could turn when he went around a corner. He fastened a pole onto the front axle, an' yoked up his oxen to it, an' had as good a wagon as he would need.

The nearest store was away off down the West Branch, where Lock Haven is today, but there warn't no Lock Haven then, just a few settlers.

Jake didn't follow down Kettle Creek to where Westport is now, because it was too far out of his way. The woods was right open, an' he tuck right off over Tamarack Mountain, up where they hit that big gas well they had such a lawsuit about, here a few years ago.

He went down Paddy Run to where Renovo is now, only there wa'n't no Renovo then, and down past Young Woman's Creek an' Quail. They called it Young Woman's Creek because some injuns had captured a young woman oncet, an' killed her an' the settlers found her body floatin' in the river right at the mouth of that creek.

Jake went on down past Lick Run, an' Queens, an' on the evenin' of the second day he got to the store, down where Lock Haven is now. He stayed a couple of days, an' bought himself some salt, an' some flour, an' some powder, an' lead to make bullets. Traded in mostly deer an' beaver skins for 'em. He didn' need no meal nor tobacco, 'cause he'd growed all he could use.

Then he started back up the West Branch, the way he'd come, drivin' along slow, 'an lettin' the oxen take their time, so's not to wear 'em out.

Along about night the second day he was gettin' up Paddy Run, but there was a good moon, an' he decided he'd try to make it on home before he slept. He'd shot a deer a little after he'd left the river, an' he was afraid the blood might attract varmints.

Now, I can't vouch for the ab-so-lute truth of what happened after that, but here's the way Jake always used to tell it:

"Hit were a-gettin' pretty dim by the time I shot the deer, an' because I couldn't see to measure out the powder I hadn't loaded up my gun. I reckoned I'd be home in a couple or three hours, anyway, an' I war gettin' anxious to see how my ol' woman had been gettin' on whilst I was away.

THE ROUTE OF JAKE WOODLEY

When Jake Woodley traveled between his cabin, on the Hammersley Fork of Kettle Creek, and Lock Haven he came through a gorge to this point. The modern highway bridge shown in the picture is immediately east of Renovo and crosses the West Branch of the Susquehanna River. Jake's cabin was approximately ten miles, as the crow flies, if he flies in a straight line, directly north (toward the horizon in the picture) from the present-day bridge in the foreground.

COMFORTABLE AND CONTENTED

"I was so tired that somehow I'd forgot that there was a terrible lot o' panthers on Tamarack.

"You know how a painter acts when he's about to jump on any kind of an animule. First he jumps down by the side of it an' walks along right in step with it: Pad! Pad! Pad!

"Well, all at oncet a great big painter jumped down by the side o' my lead ox, an' started walkin' along, Pad! Pad! Pad!

"All I had handy was my big black-snake whip, an' I was afeard to hit the varmint with it, for if he got mad there was no tellin' what he'd do. So, I up with it, an cracked it loud, right over his head. And do you know, that panther jumped right up in the wagon an' sat down beside me an' started purrin just like a pussy-cat!

"Well, I went on up pretty nigh to the top o' Tamarack, an' another painter jumped down by the side o' my off ox, an' started walkin' along, Pad! Pad! Pad! An' I cracked my whip over his head, an' he jumped in the wagon, an' started purrin' too!

"I kep' on goin', an' after I got a little way down over the top o' Tamarack, another painter jumped down by the side o' my team, an' I cracked my whip over his head, an' he jumped up in the wagon, too, an' started purrin', just like a pussy-cat!

"An' what do ye know, men, agin' I got home that night, I had a whole cart-load of purrin' panthers!"

XXII

Cherry Tree Joe McCreery

When lumbering was at its height in Clearfield, Clinton, and Lycoming Counties in Central Pennsylvania Joseph McCreery, born near Muncy, Lycoming County, became a legend, in his own lifetime. The exaggerated stories told about him before his death on November 23, 1895, at the age of 90 sound like those heard today about the mythical Paul Bunyan of the twentieth century.

McCreery moved from Lycoming County when about thirteen years of age and lived near what is now the borough of Cherry Tree, Indiana County, at the southwest corner of Clearfield County. McCreery spent much of his life rafting timber down the West Branch of the Susquehanna River, through Clearfield and Clinton Counties and his own Lycoming County.

Had it not been for an act of the General Assembly of Pennsylvania, approved April 6, 1870, we might not know of Cherry Tree Joe McCreery today. Entitled "An Act To provide for the ordinary expenses of the Government, and other general and specific appropriations," the statute was fourteen pages in length (*Laws, Session of 1870,* pages 17-30). It contained fifty-nine sections and made a large number of appropriations. The second paragraph of Section 50 stated:

> For the removal of obstructions, and the improvement of the navigation of the Susquehanna River above the line of Clinton County, the sum of three thousand dollars, to be drawn by and expended under the direction of E. B. Camp, Robert M'Kage, James B. Graham and John Patton, who shall make report of the manner of such expenditure of such sum to auditor general.°

° Navigability of the small streams tributary to the West Branch was important to lumbermen. The next year the General Assembly of Pennsylvania passed Act No. 221 "To allow the improvement of creeks and rivulets," approved March 28, 1871, pages 237-238, *Laws, Session of 1871.* The act permitted private individuals to build dams in or channels adjacent to those streams tributary to the West Branch of the Susquehanna River which had not already been declared a public highway, or clear those streams "for the purpose of floating lumber theron." Any person having this right of way in a stream was to keep his dams and other improvements in good condition, and was permitted to charge others who desired to float lumber through the improvements. The eight sections of the act were specific so as to protect the rights of land owners and lumbermen on the headwaters of the West Branch.

Chest Falls (also called Chessy) in Clearfield County, on the West Branch of the Susquehanna, was an obstruction to rafts of timber descending the river to sawmills and to market. The $3,000 appropriation was available to improve the river at Chest Falls. McCreery volunteered to remove that obstruction by dynamiting. His unsuccessful attempt to blow out the rocks is preserved in a ballad, "Cherry Tree Joe McCreery." An account in the *Cherry Tree Record* in 1890 states that the ballad was printed in about 1880 in its predecessor, the *Cherry Tree Clipper*. The ballad is also preserved in an undated broadside printed at Spangler in Cambria County, Pennsylvania, perhaps about 1890. Joseph Dudley Tonkin's *The Last Raft*, 1940, carried eight verses of the Cherry Tree Joe McCreery

A TIMBER RAFT APPROACHING THE SWIFT WATER AT CHEST FALLS ON THE WEST BRANCH OF THE SUSQUEHANNA RIVER, ABOUT 1895

From a photograph in the collections of the Clearfield County, Pennsylvania, Historical Society.

ballad (pages 71-72 and 143). Those same eight verses were repeated in George Korson's *Pennsylvania Songs and Legends*, 1949, University of Pennsylvania Press, pages 346-348. Nevertheless, Cherry Tree Joe was a forgotten figure. He and the singing of the ballad were remembered by only several elderly people.

A TIMBER RAFT ON THE UPPER REACHES OF THE WEST BRANCH OF THE SUSQUEHANNA RIVER, ABOUT 1895

From a photograph in the collections of the Clearfield County, Pennsylvania, Historical Society.

At this point the indefatigable folklorist, Dr. George Swetnam of the Pittsburgh *Press*, became interested in Joe—at or about the time he talked with Hi Cranmer and learned about those "Purring Panthers." In 1951 Swetnam's book *Pittsylvania Country*, New York, Duell, Sloan and Pearce, and later in the year an article of his in the Pittsburgh *Press* each pulled together some of the threads of the story.

The next year the October 1952 issue of *Pennsylvania History* was devoted to lumbering. Pages 461-463 reproduced the eight verses of the ballad and added a chorus of three lines. A picture of the tombstone at McCreery's grave at Cherry Tree was included.

An article by Swetnam, "Cherry Tree Joe . . . Pennsylvania's Paul Bunyan," in the Pittsburgh *Press*, October 2, 1955, carried stories about McCreery. In 1962 an article by Swetnam in the *Keystone Folklore Quarterly*, Volume VII, Number 1, Spring, "On The Trail Of Cherry Tree Joe," pages 15-33, described Joe, retold some of the tales about him, and gave the tune for the ballad. The ballad itself was documented with forty-four footnotes explaining the meaning of certain words and commenting on possible errors in the eight verses. A few months later, the Summer 1962 issue of *Keystone Folklore Quarterly* carried an editorial by Dr. Swetnam entitled, "More About Cherry Tree Joe," in which some newly discovered lines of the ballad were presented and discussed. Then on January 28 and on February 4, 1973, the Pittsburgh *Press* carried two articles by Swetnam in which he summarized his findings about the folk hero and the ballad. The articles were entitled, "Part I, On The Trail of Cherry Tree Joe," and "Part II, Cherry Tree Joe Legends." Both are reproduced here with the permission of Dr. Swetnam.

° ° ° °

Part I, On The Trail of Cherry Tree Joe

It's hard work tracking down a folk hero—even one like Cherry Tree Joe McCreery, who became a legend in his own lifetime and was celebrated in his home town.

Cherry Tree Joe was the biggest, toughest, craftiest lumberman who ever lived, and the unquestioned hero of that industry until a Minnesota advertising man invented a character named Paul Bunyan, and printed millions of pamphlets about him to advertise a lumber company.

Joe was a real man, even though a dozen men couldn't perform some of the feats credited to him. Such as the time he was racing rafts down Clearfield Creek with his old friend Bob McKeage. He was ahead, but on a straight stretch he saw the other raft was going to pass him. That wouldn't do at all.

So what did Joe do, but reach out one of his long arms to the shore, and pull out a 150-foot white pine by the roots. He swung it across and set it down, straight up, squarely in front of McKeage's raft.

That ended the race so far as Bob was concerned. But they were friends, and it didn't cause any trouble between them.

AN IMAGINATIVE SKETCH OF CHERRY TREE JOE McCREERY THE FABULOUS RAFTSMAN

The stories told about Cherry Tree Joe for a century and more varied from the feats that are possible for a big man, to things Hercules couldn't have done. And the ballad sung about him in the hills and on the rivers, pictures Joe as a great big bumbler and blowhard.

But after Paul Bunyan came along in 1914, Cherry Tree Joe was pretty well neglected. No folk hero could withstand the kind of print-pressure the Bunyan ads were pouring on.

By the time I got interested in 1949, there were a couple of books that mentioned Cherry Tree Joe, and said there were a lot of stories about him, and that he got his name from living at a place called Cherry Tree.

But there are at least two towns of that name in this area: One is in Venango County, in the Allegheny Valley, and the other in Indiana County, on the West Branch of the Susquehanna. (Besides a third in Lancaster County, and Cherry Tree Junction, in Cambria.) Nobody seemed sure which was the place in question, or whether Joe was a real man.

In 1951 I got up enough information for a story on Cherry Tree Joe. It brought me a letter from a woman who said he was a real man, and one of her ancestors. Delighted, I dashed off a letter asking which town was his home. Post haste it came back in my self-addressed envelope. Across the bottom of my letter she had written: "Yes sir, You have the right Cherry Tree Joe."

It wasn't easy to get away from the office just then, so I filed her address (as is not uncommon with me) so carefully that in over 20 years I haven't been able to find it.

Covered Meeting

That put things pretty well on ice until the fall of 1955, when I was assigned to cover the final meeting of the old Raftmen's Association, whose few members were dissolving the group. It was held at Cherry Tree, Indiana County, and after the dedication of a monument was concluded with a partial quotation from the ballad:

> " . . . The cheery hail of 'Land! Tie up!'
> to be heard no more, forever, upon these rivers."

Grasping the opportunity to make some inquiries, I quickly discovered I had found the right Cherry Tree. One or two old-timers remembered the man himself, and showed me his grave, where the tombstone said he "Died Nov. 23, 1895, past 90 years of age."

Cherry Tree Joe, it turned out, was born in 1805, near Muncy. His parents, Hugh and Nancy McCreery, brought him to Indiana County when he was about 13. He was big and strong as a youth, but quick and agile, too. Like many good athletes, he loved to show off, according to local tradition. He would make a floating log spin, just to see how well he could handle it, or "skin a cat" on a quarter line over the roughest water after the raft had tied up at Williamsport or Columbia. Some said he was more showman than worker.

"Cherry Tree Joe died when I was about 15 years old," recalled the late R. Dudley Tonkin, lumber industry historian. "I recall him as a man of maybe six foot three, weighing 200 pounds, with a beard all over his face. He's become a sort of patron saint of the lumber industry."

According to tradition, Joe was always a great ladies' man, although he married Eleanor Banks at Blairsville, perhaps while rafting on the Kiskiminetas. They had eight children, all boys, and a story about him published in 1890 said he had six grandchildren, 24 great-grandchildren, and 23 great-great-grandchildren.

In 1861—although then 56—Joe enlisted in the 11th Pennsylvania Volunteer Cavalry, and was discharged the following March, after losing a leg. After that he became short-tempered, and was sometimes called Contrary Joe.

The incident celebrated in the Cherry Tree Joe McCreery ballad occurred soon after 1871, when people of the area raised some money to relieve conditions at Chest Falls, where many rafts cracked up. Some wanted to build a dam, but Joe offered to blow out the rocks with dynamite.

He didn't know much about using it, and the result was mostly noise. But he offered to take a raft through, and wrecked it. From that time on, nearly everything that went wrong was laughingly blamed on Joe.

Cherry Tree Joe, neighbors reported, was a lifelong Methodist and Democrat. He had always hoped to go out with his boots on, but finally died in bed.

His boots were preserved, however, and for half a century were always displayed at reunions of the Raftmen's Association.

Two Big Gaps

There still remained two big gaps—the correct tune of the ballad, and the verses missing from printed copies. The song was first printed about 1880 in the "Cherry Tree Clipper."

Everyone said that the ballad was sung to either "Yankee Doodle" or "The Blue-Tail Fly," but unfortunately it won't fit either without doing great violence to the meter.

I wrote another story, giving the new facts. And right away, got a letter from Cherry Tree Joe's great-granddaughter, living at Marianna, Washington County. She said she knew the tune, and had often heard great-grandpa sing it. He liked it, even though it made fun of him.

Once more I lost the letter! And efforts to retrieve her name proved absolutely futile, for nearly 12 years. Then, one day, as I was driving in that area and saw a signpost, it suddenly popped into my memory: Mrs. Jasper Estep. She was over 75, but quite alert, and sang the ballad to a tune that did fit. It is what an expert calls "a very good folk tune in a watered-down folk tradition."

Soon afterwards, S. Arthur Boocks of Weirton, W. Va., who had learned the song from his father, came up with one missing verse, and enough of two others to permit a good guess at how they ran.

Part II, Cherry Tree Joe Legends

Cherry Tree Joe McCreery legends describe the lumber era hero as anywhere from a mere six feet, three inches, to a giant who could tie a raft to each foot and skate down the Susquehanna River to Williamsport in a day—half that if the river was frozen!

You can take your pick, or have it both ways, so long as you're dealing with legend.

Joe had a cabin somewhere in the hills of Indiana County, on The Creek Without An End, where he kept moose for milk cows, and a panther for a house cat, because the crumbs from his table were so rich that the mice grew to weigh 60 pounds. Joe's wife cooked on a griddle six feet square, and used a side of bacon to grease it and a barrel of flour every morning to make flapjacks.

Old Cherry Tree Joe was crafty, too, and drove such hard bargains that his friends said he'd "skin a flea for the hide and tallow, and stand a lawsuit in Hell for the cracklings."

One year he didn't have any white pine to raft down to Pittsburgh, so he sawed up a lot of hemlock, and rafted it, instead. That was the first hemlock anyone had ever tried to sell in the town, and he told a buyer it was "knot pine." By the time he was back here again, the dealer had discovered his mistake (hemlock wasn't worth half as much as pine) and was hopping mad. Cherry Tree Joe wasn't ruffled at all. "Don't you remember?" he said. "The first thing I told you when you asked about the raft was: 'It's not pine.' "

Joe was so strong he could shoulder five bushels of shot. But when he tried to carry it on a bet, he mired up to his knees in a flint rock. His eyes were so sharp that he could take a raft down a river in pitch darkness.

Heard For Miles

When rafting, he never needed to carry lights or a fog horn, for when he sang or whistled he could be heard three miles. Joe didn't have many enemies, but for those few, it made their hair fall out, just to think of him.

Whenever a raft would get jammed on a rock, snag or dam, instead of using dynamite, the rivermen would just call for Cherry Tree Joe. He'd straighten things out.

One time he single-handedly broke a 10-mile log jam at Buttermilk Falls; and once at the famous Gerry's Rocks he just lifted a timber raft clear, set it down in safe water, and jumped aboard.

One time, though, some raftmen who had asked for help got a real surprise. It was a bad jam, and the whole raft was made of birch logs. While studying just how to get the matter straightened out, Joe pulled out his knife and began whittling. Before he realized it, he had cut the whole raft into little sticks—and that's how toothpicks were invented. He loaded them onto a flatboat and took them to Philadelphia, where the people were so delighted they paid him $5,000 more than the raft had been worth.

Called His Bluff

Returning from the Philadelphia trip, he called John L. Sullivan's bluff in Dwyer's Hotel at Renovo, and slapped the champion's wrist.

At John Eisel's tavern at Snowshoe, where he had stopped for a drink ("Water's only for women an' babies," he used to say) he picked up a broad-axe and whacked off the tail of an organ-grinder's monkey. The animal jumped up on the bar, and he and Joe bombarded one another with bottles until the place was a shambles.

But without a doubt, Joe's most remembered real exploit, which gave rise to his ballad, was his biggest failure.

In 1871 Pennsylvania passed a law permitting private persons to make improvements on small, nonnavigable streams, and recover the cost by charging tolls to those who used them. Usually these were either chutes, which drove most of the water to one side, making it deep enough for rafts, or splash dams. These were used to impound water, usually on small sidestreams, to be released when needed for rafts or flatboats.

At Chest Falls, near Mahaffy, the rocky bottom often caused rafts to go aground or break up. Two lumbermen, Bob McKeague and E. B. Camp, advanced money to remedy the situation.

There was considerable discussion, but Cherry Tree Joe insisted the best thing to do was blow out the big rocks. They bought a box of dynamite,

THE LAST TIMBER RAFT ON THE WEST BRANCH OF THE SUSQUEHANNA RIVER, 1938

A reminder of the raftsmen of Central Pennsylvania in the last half of the nineteenth century, among whom Cherry Tree Joe McCreery was king and giant. From the frontispiece of **The Last Raft**, *1940, by Joseph Dudley Tonkin, with Mr. Tonkin's permission.*

THE LAST RAFT GOING OVER THE LOCK HAVEN DAM, 1938
From a photograph in the collections of the Clearfield County, Pennsylvania, Historical Society.

which none of them knew how to use, but McCreery volunteered.

"On the way out," reported the late Dudley Tonkin, who heard it from his father, "they stopped at John Patchin's store, and talked his son Jack out of a gallon of whisky. The blasting made lots of noise, but moved mighty little rock. The falls were as big a hazard as ever, and whenever a raft wrecked there everybody blamed Cherry Tree Joe."

Words and tune alike, the ballad of Cherry Tree Joe McCreery is one of the most honestly original folk productions of the Pittsylvania Country.

The air, although showing some kinship to others, is as truly individual as any to be found here, while the words—continually filled with personal and place names—are the genuine work of some local troubadour.

Most of the people mentioned are easy to trace: Bob McKeage, E. B. Camp, Robert Porter, James Dowler, prominent lumbermen of the 1870s; James Riddle, a dealer, have proved easier to locate in history than McCreery

Places mentioned—Chest (or Chessy) Falls, Sliding Point, Rocky Bend, are all close to Cherry Tree, named for a landmark that went back to early pioneer days. Even the slang and reference to a cooperative effort at clearing the upper channel of the Susquehanna's West Branch, are genuine. Conjectural lines for those missing are in parentheses.

1. You rivermen have surely heard about the appropriation
   That was made to clear our little ditch and benefit the nation.
   That we might run through Chessy Falls nor get the least bit weary.
   So they raised the stamps and gave the job to Cherry Tree Joe McCreery.

Refrain:
   Lookin' out for number one; Spendin' all the money,
   And gettin' nothin' done.

2. There's Bob McKeage and E. B. Camp who held the ready ginger.
   Some men of sense said, "Build a dam," but they'd not raise a finger.
   We'll blow the rocks skyhigh said they, "so Porter don't get skeery.
   (The very man to do the job is Cherry Tree Joe McCreery.)"

3. (Joe quickly came up with a plan for our consideration.)
   He'd blow our little river out with the vast appropriation.
   (Twould make a noise that all would hear from Somerset to Erie.
   "I'll blow her out or bust your ear," says Cherry Tree Joe McCreery.

4. The job being done, old Joe came home and did some heavy blowing.
   He swore he'd put a long raft through, and do but little rowing.
   "Don't hold her up to Sliding Point, or get the least bit skeery,
   But let her rip and she'll go through," says Cherry Tree Joe McCreery.

5. (He wrecked the raft and took t' th' woods just where he'd sure leave no trail;)
   I b'lieve a game of dominoes could've been played on his coat tail.
   (To face his fellows of our town he seemed a little leery.
   But two weeks later, sneakin' home come Cherry Tree Joe McCreery.)

6. Now you all know, and I can show that fate's a cruel master.
   When once you're going down the hill, he's sure to push you faster.
   And that's the way—mind what I say—and don't you see, my dearie,
   That everything that happens now is blamed on Joe McCreery.

7. One day last spring, as I come up, I met somebody's daughter,
   Who held her apron to her eyes to catch the salty water.
   "Dear girl," said I, "what makes you cry? You must feel very dreary."
   "Why, my daddy stoved in Chessy Falls, and I'm huntin' Joe McCreery."

8. The other day they had a splash, and jammed her tight as thunder.
   A circumstance that caused our folks to gaze around in wonder.
   They prayed and tore, ripped and swore, until they all grew weary.
   Sheff cut his bill raft into sticks, and cursed old Joe McCreery.

9. Now Captain Dowler, t'other day, he struck a raft of timber.
   That was hanging up on Sliding Point, and tore the rope asunder.
   The captain winked and scratched his head, saying, "This is kind of dreary."
   Then jumped his oar, went on shore, and prayed for Joe McCreery.

10. Our Squire Riddle on the hill, who deals out justice even—
    His head is very bald, you know, no hair 'twixt him and heaven.
    I asked him why his hair came out; he answered to my query:
    "It just came out, thinkin' about Cherry Tree Joe McCreery."

11. In years to come, when no rafts run on our dear little river.
    And the cheery cry of "Land! Tie up!" is heard no more, forever,
    Down Rocky Bend and through Chest Falls, on winter nights so eerie,
    The phantom raftmen will chase the ghost of Cherry Tree Joe McCreery.

INDEX